BASIC
COMPUTING
SCIENCE

Data Structures

BASIC
COMPUTING
SCIENCE

Data
Structures

Brian Bailey B.Sc.

Educational Computer Centre,
London Borough of Havering

BLACKIE

Basic Computing Science
General Editor: W. R. Broderick

System Software	Peter J. Barker
Logic and Arithmetic in Computing	John Jaworski
Data Structures	Brian Bailey
Approaches to Programming	Brian Jackson
Development of Computer-Based Systems	Gail and Paul Sealey
Computer Architecture	Harold Wise

ISBN 0 216 90856 6

First published 1980

Published by Blackie & Son Ltd
Bishopbriggs, Glasgow G64 2NZ
Furnival House, 14–18 High Holborn, London WC1V 6BX

Filmset by Willmer Brothers Limited, Merseyside

Printed in Great Britain by Thomson Litho Limited, East Kilbride

General Editor's Foreword

Computing science is concerned with the processing of information and as such is one of the most fundamental sciences in our society today. This series provides a modern approach to computing science at a level suitable for introductory courses in schools, colleges and universities. It concentrates upon the fundamentals of the subject and provides a strong foundation from which further studies may develop. Both the principles and the practice of the subject are covered. The texts concentrate upon data structures and the ways in which computers manipulate data. Processors and peripherals are seen as tools used for collecting and processing data. Thus, there is reference to computers in terms of their logic, architecture and characteristics but there is no undue concentration upon details of how particular pieces of equipment work. A knowledge of the fundamentals of programming is essential to computing science and the emphasis in this series is upon the concepts rather than on the detailed explanation of modes of operation. Programming practice is considered an essential element of data processing and where necessary and desirable, the texts are illustrated with examples in common computing languages.

Students working at this level find it necessary to relate the theory to practice, and opportunities are taken to illustrate the algorithms and practices derived from the theoretical study. The problems of high volume data processing operations and other applications are discussed.

Whilst the approach is academic it is related to the practice of computing wherever possible. It is aimed (in the United Kingdom) at GCE Advanced Level and at First Year Higher Education Service Courses but the breadth and depth of coverage is such as to make the series immediately useful to those with a serious interest in computing science and its practice.

Data Structures concentrates upon the relationship between information, data and structure—one of the fundamental concepts of computing science. This book is therefore kernel to the series. It surveys data structures and their associated mapping functions ranging from one-dimensional arrays through to tree structures, and looks at applications of these in a computing context.

Whilst the text is academic, the style and presentation are easy and readable. Clearly written algorithms of how to build and access the various data structures considered are given, making this book an important reference text for practitioners, teachers and students alike. By starting from the concept of encoding information, progressing through data structures and finishing with a simple treatment of syntax analysis, this text illustrates Brian Bailey's command of his subject.

W. R. Broderick

Author's Foreword

After working with teachers and students for several years I came to realize that many people are unable to distinguish between information and data. It soon transpires that these 'unenlightened' ones have taken the existence of data structures for granted. It seems a pity that these people frequently use data structuring facilities within high-level programming languages yet they know very little about how or why data structures work. So, it is to these 'unenlightened' ones that I dedicate this book in the hope that it might help them see the light.

The recurring theme of this book is
$$INFORMATION \equiv DATA + STRUCTURE$$
Whilst we are primarily interested in the formation and use of data structures in their various forms, an attempt has been made to make the reader aware that data is not always of a numeric nature.

The data structures described range from arrays, through lists and on to the ubiquitous tree structure in its various forms, including its use in networks and syntax analysis. Throughout the text the uses of these structures are described by way of examples and diagrams.

Each chapter has a similar format; an introduction to the structure and its uses, a detailed description of the structure in its various forms, a summary and a set of exercises. Included within the description of each structure are algorithms, written in English, describing how the structures concerned can be manipulated.

It is hoped that this text will be used for both a teaching text and as a reference for teachers and students alike. Chapters 2, 3, 4 and 5 should be covered in the order they appear in the book because they contain a discussion of the 'pros' and 'cons' of each of the structures described. This 'discussion' is a pre-requisite to Chapters 6 and 7 which can be read independently of one another.

The algorithms that appear within the text will, hopefully, be of some value to those readers who wish to implement the structures within a a computer system. In such cases the reader will find the combination of this text with another publication in this series, *Approaches to Programming* by Brian Jackson, of great value.

I wish to thank the University of London, University Entrance and School Examinations Council; the Associated Examining Board; and the University of Cambridge Local Examinations Syndicate for permission to reproduce questions from past examinations.

This foreword would not be complete without a few words of thanks to Christine Nutman who had the unenviable task of translating my handwriting into a legible manuscript.

Finally, I would like to thank my wife Elaine for her patience and understanding during the writing of this book.

Brian Bailey

Contents

1 Encoding Information

This chapter is a discussion of the problems involved in presenting information to a computer system, and in retrieving information from the same computer system.

1.1 Symbols and conventions

The string of symbols you are reading at the moment has some meaning to you. It is assumed you have acquired the skill of reading. However, ask yourself these questions: 'How do I know that these symbols on a page mean something?' and, 'What are they doing there in the first place?'

To answer the second question first, let us go back several thousand years. Out of pride and perhaps vanity, man communicated to his peers information about his achievements. At first this was done by drawing pictures on cave walls. As years went by, perhaps man realized how long it took to draw these pictures and decided upon some form of shorthand. This shorthand has evolved over the years to the symbols you see today.

The most important point to be made here is that when man evolved from cave drawings to writing with symbols, he had to decide on a set of rules for the interpretation of these symbols, so that their meaning could be recognized by his contemporaries.

So, to answer our original questions, we write symbols on a page to communicate information to one another, and the only reason the recipient of the symbols understands is because a common convention of interpretation exists.

Not all our ancestors agreed upon the same set of symbols (for cultural and geographical reasons) and hence the existence today of a large number of sets of symbols. Similarly, even after conventions for symbols have been agreed upon, man has used a multitude of conventions to interpret combinations of these symbols, producing English, French, etc.

Consequently, we arrive at the conclusion that information can only be conveyed if the recipient recognizes the symbols used, and is capable of interpreting the groups of symbols under a convention agreed with the sender.

1.2 Data

To many people, the word 'data' means a set of numbers, for example:

$$365 \quad 17 \quad -10 \quad 63$$

What must be realized is that the *data* above is only data, and not *information*, until we are given a set of rules or a convention under which we can interpret the data.

Normally we might assume that the data above is representing numbers to base ten, but this is only so because numbers to base ten play such an important part in our lives. On closer examination though, the data

$$365 \quad 17 \quad -10 \quad 63$$

could represent numbers to base eight, base nine, base ten, base eleven and so on. The data might not even represent numbers at all. Hence we must be told the structure or convention under which information is encoded to produce data.

The word 'data' is not the sole property of the world of numbers. For example, the following string of characters is data.

MARY HAD A LITTLE LAMB

It is only when the conventions with regard to the structure of words and sentences in English are applied to the above data that information appears.

From the above observations we can derive a maxim:

$$INFORMATION \equiv DATA + STRUCTURE$$

When the grammar of English sentences is applied to data like that above, sentences are produced. The rules of English grammar are called *production rules*, because they produce sentences.

In the following example, the syntactic elements are enclosed within

'<' and '>'. The string of characters mentioned above, MARY HAD A LITTLE LAMB, form a sentence, S, when the following production rules are applied:

```
                      <sentence>
Rule 1:     <subject noun> <verb phrase>
Rule 2:     <subject noun> <verb> <object phrase>
Rule 3:     <subject noun> <verb> <article> <object>
Rule 4:     <subject noun> <verb> <article> <adjective> <object noun>
Rule 5:     MARY          <verb> <article> <adjective> <object noun>
Rule 6:     MARY          HAD    <article> <adjective> <object noun>
Rule 7:     MARY          HAD    A         <adjective> <object noun>
Rule 8:     MARY          HAD    A         LITTLE      <object noun>
Rule 9:     MARY          HAD    A         LITTLE      LAMB
```

It is common practice when forming production rules to use the following conventions:

1. Lower case letters of the alphabet e.g. a, b, c, etc., are used to denote the *terminal symbols* of the final language, like MARY and LITTLE in our example above.
2. Upper case letters of the alphabet e.g. A, B, C, etc., called *non-terminal symbols*, are used to denote non-terminal expressions like <verb phrase> in our example above.
3. Lower case Greek letters such as α, β, γ, etc., are used to denote strings of symbols both terminal and non-terminal.

Consequently, the set of production rules in our example for sentence S is as follows:

```
        Rule 1:     S→aB
        Rule 2:     B→cD
        Rule 3:     D→eF
        Rule 4:     F→gh
        Rule 5:     a→MARY
        Rule 6:     c→HAD
        Rule 7:     e→A
        Rule 8:     g→LITTLE
        Rule 9:     h→LAMB
```

The set of production rules shown here is just a small subset of those required for all forms of an English sentence. The complete set of production rules for a given language is called the *grammar* of the language.

It is important to remember that production rules exist for other types of data. For instance, suppose a computer manufacturer wishes to be able to reference each of his many products by a unique index. The product index must contain the following items:

1. A three letter mnemonic to indicate the factory of origin of the product.
2. A three digit number to indicate the product number.
3. A single letter A-Z to denote the option available with the product.

The production rules below are applied to the data XYZ159P.

```
                <product index>
Rule 1:     <factory mnemonic> <product number> <option code>
Rule 2:     XYZ                <product number> <option code>
Rule 3:     XYZ                159              <option code>
Rule 4:     XYZ                159              P
```

This set of production rules or grammar to produce a product index, I, can be represented in a shortened form like this:

```
        Rule 1:     I→abc
        Rule 2:     a→XYZ
        Rule 3:     b→159
        Rule 4:     c→P
```

1.3 Chomsky language classification types

Various attempts have been made to classify languages; the work of Chomsky (1959) is the best known. We shall be concentrating on his study of artificial languages. Chomsky put forward the idea that all artificial languages could be classified into four types (0, 1, 2 and 3). Each of his language types is a subset of its predecessor.

Chomsky Type 0 language

The production rules for this type of language take the form $\alpha \to \beta$ which provide too wide a scope for computer programming languages yet they are too restricting for natural languages such as English. Consequently, this language type proves to be too general to be of much use when dealing with artificial languages.

Chomsky Type 1 language

This language type is used to define context-sensitive languages where the production rules are limited to the form $\alpha A \beta \rightarrow \alpha \gamma \beta$ where α, β are empty or strings of symbols, and where γ is always a string of symbols.

Chomsky Type 2 language

This is perhaps the most commonly occurring language type. The production rules are of the form $A \rightarrow \gamma$ where γ is a string of symbols. Hopefully, the reader will have noticed that this is the special case of a Type 1 language where α and β are empty.

Most programming languages can be said to be of Chomsky Type 2 classification. For instance, the programming language ALGOL is defined in Backus* Normal Form (BNF) which itself is a Chomsky Type 2 language.

Chomsky Type 3 language

The production rules for this classification appear in the form

$$A \rightarrow a \text{ or } A \rightarrow bB$$

This language classification and its predecessor, Type 2, provide facilities for the repeated use of a production rule by itself. For example, the production rules to define a string S, of a's of any length greater than or equal to one are as follows:

Rule 1:	$S \rightarrow a$
Rule 2:	$S \rightarrow aS$

If the string 'aaa' were to be produced, production rule 2 would be applied twice to allow the definition of string S to take place as shown below:

	S
Rule 2:	aS
Rule 2:	aaS
Rule 1:	aaa

This occurrence is known as recursion and is a technique used extensively

*Sometimes known as Backus-Naur Form.

in computer science. A further example of the use of recursion can be seen with the Chomsky Type 2 language below.

The following set of production rules define the grammar for a language of all the arithmetic expressions, E, formed from the letters p and q and the operators + and ×.

Rule 1:	$E \rightarrow p$
Rule 2:	$E \rightarrow q$
Rule 3:	$E \rightarrow p\gamma$
Rule 4:	$E \rightarrow q\gamma$
Rule 5:	$\gamma \rightarrow +E$
Rule 6:	$\gamma \rightarrow \times E$

The production rules used to define the expression p+q are as follows:

	E
Rule 3:	$p\gamma$
Rule 5:	$p+E$
Rule 2:	$p+q$

Even for this simple expression, p+q, to be produced, recursion has to take place to allow for the definition of E in production rule 5.

Further examples of the use of recursion are discussed in later chapters of this book.

1.4 Processing data

One of the main criticisms levelled at some computer systems is that the data output is insufficient for man to interpret and build a complete information picture of the problem at hand. For example, perhaps the output produced is just a set of digits with no character strings to describe what the digits represent. This could be the description (or lack of description) of errors detected during the compilation of a program. Alternatively, certain characteristics of the source information have not been highlighted.

It is very often the case that when information is encoded to form data some information is lost along the way. Sometimes the structure used fails to produce data which represents the information completely or accurately. For instance, if the data

HE CANNOT WALK WITHOUT USING WALKING STICKS

is subjected to the grammar of the English language, the resulting information tells us that a male person is unable to walk unless he can use walking sticks to help him.

If, however, the data is changed, perhaps to reduce its length, the new form of the data could be:

HE CAN WALK USING WALKING STICKS

The resulting information tells us that a male person can walk using walking sticks but there is no implication, as there was before, that without the walking sticks he is unable to walk at all.

Here we have a situation where the source data has been amended, or perhaps encoded, resulting in a corruption of the original information. Consequently, the computer system cannot be expected to perform miracles and make sense out of incomplete or inaccurate data. Remember that information is not processed but its data representation is.

The fault lies in two possible areas; the encoding of information to produce the input data, and the inability of the programmer and/or computer system to cope with the demands of the project.

In Chapter 1 of *Logic and Arithmetic in Computing* by John Jaworski, we see that a computer system can receive as input data a string of digits, build a number from these digits, and store the number away in its memory.Similarly, a computer system can receive as input data a string of symbols such as characters of the alphabet, digits, punctuation marks and mathematical signs. Just as the computer system has an algorithm for dealing with digits so it has an algorithm for looking after symbol strings.

There are internationally agreed conventions on how data should be represented on paper tape, punched card and magnetic tape. As a result, computer systems have some means of interpreting these representations, but what the computer system does internally with the resulting bit patterns varies according to the unit of storage in the system. Some computer systems have facilities for manipulating individual characters; they are usually represented with eight bits.

Many computer systems leave the structuring of data inside the system to the programmer or systems analyst, which leaves the ball very much on the programmer's side of the net. Hopefully, a good programmer or systems analyst will use data structures which show accurately all the relationships between the data and allow this data to be accessed and

modified efficiently. If the data structure does not accurately portray the relationships between the items of data then the original information has been corrupted and output from the computer system should be regarded with suspicion.

This brings us back to our maxim:

INFORMATION ≡ DATA + STRUCTURE

where the implementation of the data structure plays such an important part.

Summary

The moral of the story so far could well be 'take nothing for granted'.

Remember that the data is not truly representative of information until the correct structure or convention has been applied.

This correct structure or convention must be described in an unambiguous fashion itself so that misinterpretation does not take place; hence the need for production rules and the classification of language types by Chomsky.

It is hoped that after reading this book, the reader will have an insight into how structures can be set up within a computer system to represent information faithfully.

EXERCISES
1. *The designer of a programming language defines the representation of a 'fractional number' externally to the computer in the following words:*

   'an optional + or − sign followed by at least one denary digit, followed by an obligatory decimal point, followed by any number (including none) of digits.'

Thus,

   123.45   +123.45   0.123 and 123.

are all examples of legal fractional numbers, while

   +.5   123   .5 and .0

are not acceptable.

Using the definitions

$$<digit> \rightarrow 0|1|2|3|4|5|6|7|8|9$$
$$<sign> \rightarrow +|-$$

write production rules that formally define *<fractional number>* as described above. *(LONDON 1975)*.

2. Define the grammar for a language *(Chomsky Type 2)* which consists of a string of a's and b's followed by their mirror image, e.g. *aababbabaa.*

3. The following production rules define the syntax of an expression:

$$<expression> ::= <term>|<sign> \qquad <term>|<expression>$$
$$<operator> \quad <term>$$
$$<term> ::= <constant>|<variable*(expression)>$$
$$<operator> ::= +|-|*|/$$

$<sign> ::= +|-$
$<variable> ::= <letter>|<variable><letter>$
$<constant> ::= <digit>|<constant><digit>$
$<letter> ::= A|B|C|D|E|F|G|H|I|J|K|L|M|N|O|P|Q|R|S|$
$\qquad T|U|V|W|X|Y|Z$
$<digit> ::= 0|1|2|3|4|5|6|7|8|9$

Copy any of the following which are not expressions, indicating at which point in the string of characters failure is detected (assuming a left to right scan), thus:

$$2HB$$
$$\uparrow$$

(i) A1–3 (ii) RHUBARB (iii) ITEM–2 (iv) A/B/C (v) 2
(vi) –(+(0)) (vii) *B (viii) Y+3.2 (ix) 2/0 (x) (A–(B–2)
(xi) P (2)*

(Cambridge Specimen Paper)

2 Arrays

Computer systems can deal quite happily with single items of data, but when related pieces of data are to be processed then the writers of computer software have to devise suitable structures so that the relationships can be maintained inside a computer system. One of the basic structures used to store related pieces of data is an *array*. High-level programming languages such as COBOL, FORTRAN and BASIC have facilities available for using arrays, whilst low-level languages leave the programmer to devise his or her own structure for storing these related pieces of data.

This chapter describes how arrays are used, how individual data items within an array can be accessed, and how to get the best out of an array structure.

2.1 The use of arrays

The concept of using arrays as a means of storing data inside a computer system is taken from the arena of mathematics.

A set of related variables $b_1, b_2, b_3, \ldots, b_n$ can be described as a vector $\boldsymbol{b}$ of size n.

From this mathematical concept can be drawn the idea of an array B in which can be stored related pieces of data.

Suppose the number of articles produced each day by Bob, a machine operator in a factory, are to be stored inside a computer system. During a particular week Bob's production figures are as follows: Monday 63, Tuesday 43, Wednesday 57, Thursday 61 and Friday 51. The data could be stored in a computer system under an identifier B as shown in Fig. 1. Each day's production can be accessed individually, for example, Wednesday's production can be accessed by referring to B(3) and Monday's by B(1). In other words, a structure exists:

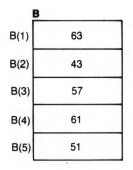

Fig. 1 Production figures for a machine operator, stored in an array B.

all Bob's production figures can be found under the identifier B and each day's production can be found in particular places in the array. This particular array is called a *one-dimensional array* because its diagrammatic representation (Fig. 1) stretches in one dimension only.

Suppose now that the production figures of two more machine operators, Jenny 43, 62, 59, 71 and 59, and Carol 49, 75, 60, 57 and 55, are to be added to the computer system. Working along the same lines as before, this would cause Jenny's production figures to be stored in an array J and Carol's in array C as shown in Fig. 2.

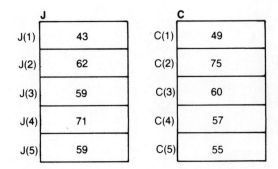

Fig. 2 Production figures for two more machine operators.

If a program were to be written to perform some statistical analysis on Tuesday's production figures of our three machine operators, you can see that references would have to be made in the program to B(2), J(2) and C(2) because we know that all Tuesday's production figures are held in position 2 in each of our three arrays. As you can see, the programmer's job is made quite complex even with just three machine operators because three different identifiers, B, J and C have to be referenced. Imagine the difficulties of dealing with the production figures of a large number of machine operators.

We soon come to realize that, whilst the one-dimensional array has its uses, it becomes restrictive when attempting to deal with large amounts of data. One possible solution to the problem is to use a *two-dimensional array*. If we take the production figures of our three machine operators Bob, Jenny and Carol, we can enter them into a two-dimensional array S as shown in Fig. 3 where Bob's production figures occupy the first column, Jenny's the second and Carol's the third. The production figures relating to each day remain in the same row position in S as they did for their respective one-dimensional arrays B, J and C. For example, Jenny's production figure for Wednesday (59) can be found in the third row and second column of S, and is hence referenced as S(3,2).

It is a convention that the elements of two-dimensional arrays, i.e. the individual items of data, are always referenced by row and then by

S	Bob	Jenny	Carol
Monday	63	43	49
Tuesday	43	62	75
Wednesday	57	59	60
Thursday	61	71	57
Friday	51	59	55

Fig. 3   The production figures for the three machine operators can be stored in a two-dimensional array S.

column. The row number and column number are known as the *subscripts* of the element.

So, if we go back to our problem of analysing Tuesday's production figures of our machine operators, Bob, Jenny and Carol, we can now reference their production figures by S(2,1), S(2,2) and S(2,3) respectively, which makes the programmer's life a little easier.

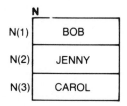

Fig. 4   The names of the three machine operators could be stored in a one-dimensional array N.

In our example we have dealt with data solely of a numeric form. When dealing with character strings the principles involved in one-and two-dimensional arrays are the same as those for numbers. For example, the names of the machine operators whose production figures are held in array S could be stored under a one-dimensional array structure N as shown in Fig. 4. Notice as before, that each item of data can be referenced uniquely, e.g. CAROL is referenced by N(3) because this data is found in the third element of array N. Notice also that the subscript in this case, 3, is the column in the two-dimensional array S (Fig. 3) in which the production figures for Carol are found.

With one-dimensional and two-dimensional arrays we can represent some relationships between items of data. Some computer systems, but not all, allow the programmer to use arrays with more than two dimensions so that more complex relationships can be represented.

2.2   Storage of arrays

When arrays are represented inside a computer system's memory they are usually mapped into vectors. This means that a two-dimensional array is mapped into a single vector with its elements occupying contiguous memory locations.

This mapping into a single vector can be performed in more than one way. For example, the data held in the two-dimensional array S in Fig. 3 could be mapped row-by-row to give Fig. 5 or alternatively column-by-column to give Fig. 6.

(1,1)	(1,2)	(1,3)	(2,1)	(2,2)	(2,3)	(3,1)	(3,2)	(3,3)	(4,1)	(4,2)	(4,3)	(5,1)	(5,2)	(5,3)
63	43	49	43	62	75	57	59	60	61	71	57	51	59	55

Fig. 5   The two-dimensional array S mapped row-by-row to give a single vector.

(1,1)	(2,1)	(3,1)	(4,1)	(5,1)	(1,2)	(2,2)	(3,2)	(4,2)	(5,2)	(1,3)	(2,3)	(3,3)	(4,3)	(5,3)
63	43	57	61	51	43	62	59	71	59	49	75	60	57	55

Fig. 6   Column-by-column mapping of S.

Just as there is more than one method for mapping a two-dimensional array into a single vector, there is more than one method for accessing the array elements which now exist inside the computer system's memory.

2.3   Accessing array elements with dope vectors

When a programmer wishes to use an array structure in FORTRAN a declaration has to be made. For example:

DIMENSION IOPR(3,5)

This causes certain information to be made available to the computer system; a two-dimensional array is to be represented with known upper and lower bounds and a known number of elements. This information is represented in a *dope vector*.

The declaration for IOPR might cause the FORTRAN compiler to produce two pointers associated with the identifier IOPR. The first to the start address of the vector containing the array elements, and the second to the dope vector mentioned above.

Using the dope vector and the start address of the vector containing the array elements it is possible to access each element of an array. Let us take the simple case of a one-dimensional array and then adapt our model for use with a two-dimensional array.

The one-dimensional array B in Fig. 1 could have its start address denoted by B_a so that the memory locations of elements B(1), B(2), B(3), B(4) and B(5) are B_a, B_{a+1}, B_{a+2}, B_{a+3} and B_{a+4} respectively.

The memory address MB(i) of element B(i) can be obtained from the mapping function.

$$MB(i) = B_{a+i-1}$$

Taking our model further, we can find a mapping function for two-dimensional arrays. The two-dimensional array S represented in Fig. 3 can, as we have seen, be mapped into the vectors represented in Fig. 5 and Fig. 6. It has also been mentioned that the dope vector for a particular array holds such information as the upper and lower bounds of each dimension of an array. We will denote the row upper bound by m, the column upper bound by n, and the lower bounds will be assumed to be equal to one.

The start address of the mapping of array S in Fig. 5 and Fig. 6 will be denoted by S_a.

The memory address MS(ij) of element S(i,j) can be obtained from the mapping function

$$MS(ij) = S_{a+n(i-1)+j-1}$$

for the row-by-row mapping of array S in Fig. 5. Similarly, the mapping function

$$MS(ij) = S_{a+m(j-1)+i-1}$$

can be used to determine the memory address MS(ij) of element S(i,j) for the column-by-column mapping of array S in Fig. 6.

These mapping functions are used every time an array element is accessed during the execution of a program. Most compilers would at this time implement some form of array-bound check using the information held in the array's dope vector. Consequently, whenever an element of an array is to be accessed its memory address is calculated using the appropriate mapping function which makes use of the data in the dope vector and the subscripts of the element.

2.4 Array accessing with Iliffe vectors

A faster method of accessing array elements is that using *Iliffe vectors*. Against this, however, is the fact that this method requires more computer memory than the method described previously.

When each array used is mapped into a vector, a set of pointers in the

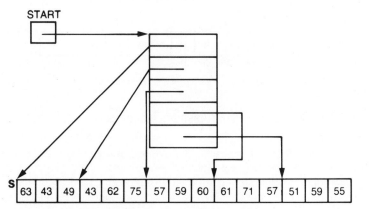

Fig. 7   Iliffe vector accessing the row-by-row mapping of S.

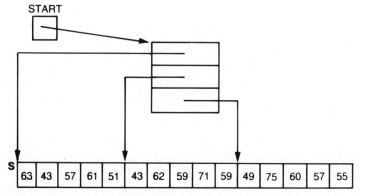

Fig. 8   Iliffe vector accessing the column-by-column mapping of S.

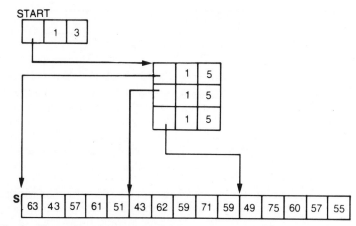

Fig. 9   The upper and lower bounds of each array subscript can be stored with each Iliffe vector element.

form of a vector is created. These pointers contain the actual storage locations of the data they point to. No calculation is required for this method, only the following of pointers. For example, Fig. 7 shows an Iliffe vector with its pointers to the row-by-row mapping of the two-dimensional array S (Fig. 3). When array S is mapped column-by-column, and an Iliffe vector is used to access the elements, the representation is as shown in Fig. 8. Notice that the second representation requires less computer memory yet the same information has been represented.

One drawback of our representations so far has been the absence of array-bound checking facilities. This can be overcome by storing the upper and lower bounds of each subscript with each Iliffe vector element as in Fig. 9.

2.5 Access tables

The ideas of Iliffe (as we have seen) can be used when dealing with numeric data. However, the same principles can be used for data in the guise of character strings.

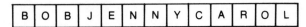

Fig. 10 *Vector representation of array N (Fig. 4).*

In an earlier example in this chapter we took the names of three machine operators, Bob, Jenny and Carol and entered these names as data in an array N (Fig. 4). As we have said before, arrays are represented in computer memory as vectors so the representation in Fig. 4 would become Fig. 10. How do we access each element of array N now represented in Fig. 10? This can be done by introducing an access table A containing the addresses of the first character of each element as shown in Fig. 11.

When dealing with the storage of numeric data it is often the case that numbers are stored in units of memory; the size of this unit may vary, however, from computer system to computer system. Strings have totally different characteristics mainly because they can be of varying lengths. Consequently, whilst it is possible to access the start of each string in Fig. 11 there is no means of telling where each string finishes.

A second vector L is now required to contain the lengths of each character string. Used properly this vector L would prevent over-running from one string to the next. Fig. 12 shows the arrangement.

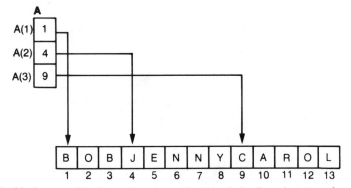

Fig. 11 *Access table A contains the addresses of the first character of each element in array N.*

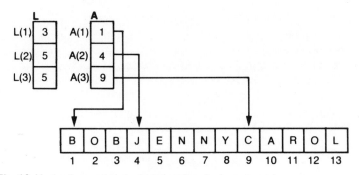

Fig. 12 *Vector L contains the lengths of each character string.*

2.6 Array accessing using hashing functions

One of the limitations in the use of access tables is that there must be a one-to-one relationship between the number of possible data items to be accessed and the storage locations available. To illustrate this disadvantage, imagine storing information concerning bank accounts in a computer system. If the details of each bank account can be referenced through a unique number of eight digits, the maximum number of accounts would be $10^8 - 1$ assuming zero is an invalid account number. This unique number is called a *key*.

Obviously, if access tables are used a very large number of pointers have to exist, many of which are unused at any given time. A method called *hash addressing* allows us to perform the same task without the need for a large number of pointers. The method works on the principle that for every key K_i there is an address A_i where the key K_i and its associated data are stored. Each address A_i is a function of the key K_i such that

$$A_i = f(K_i)$$

A suitable function must be selected to give an even distribution of addresses for A_i within the memory space available.

To illustrate the use of this method consider the following example. Suppose the details of people's bank accounts were to be stored in a computer system. Each bank account can be referenced uniquely by a positive four digit number (excluding zero) and the bank never has more than 1000 customers at any given time. Each bank account number or key submitted to the computer system must be made available to a hashing function. There are many hashing functions in existence, all of which, hopefully, are tailored to suit their environment. We shall describe the use of just one.

The key submitted, K_i, will be integer-divided by the maximum number of keys that can be held in the computer system. The remainder from this division will give us the hash address of the key K_i and its associated data.

For example, the key 1979 will be divided by 1000, as this is the number of bank accounts to be held in the computer system, to give a remainder of 979. The key 1979 and its associated data will be stored at address 979. Using the same principle, the key 8045 and its data will be stored at address 45, as shown in Fig. 13.

The above technique can be used for storing and accessing previously stored data. However, the system does seem to fall apart when two keys appear to try to access the same storage location. For example, keys 1066 and 7066, when submitted to the hashing function, both produce the address location 66. This situation is called a *collision* of keys. The problem is overcome by introducing overflow tables which contain the keys and their data which have overflowed the main storage area. Consequently, if the details of bank account number 1066 were

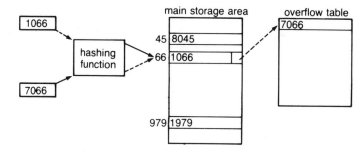

Fig. 14 An overflow table overcomes the problem of collision of keys.

stored first, the details of account number 7066 could be found in the overflow table linked by a pointer in the main storage area as shown in Fig. 14.

If there was further contention for address 66 in the main storage area by the introduction of account number 9066 then the details concerning account 9066 would be held in the overflow table and chained by a pointer from the entry made for account 7066 as in Fig. 15.

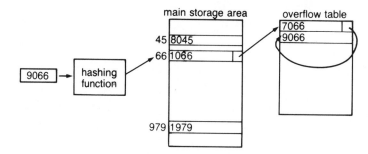

Fig. 15 Multiple collisions can be accommodated.

Summary

This chapter has described the array structure, some possible uses, and its implementation. The sections covering the accessing of elements will,

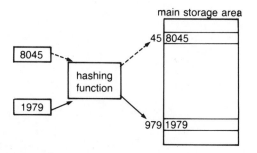

Fig. 13 Using hash addressing.

hopefully, give the reader some ideas for his own implementation of arrays.

The reader will find that the more complex structures described in later chapters such as lists, trees and networks, can be implemented on a computer system using the array as an environment in which to build these more complex structures. Consequently, the humble array, despite its inadequacies as a structure in its own right, provides facilities for more able structures.

EXERCISES

1. *Only the non-zero elements of a sparse matrix are stored sequentially in computer memory to save storage space. Devise a method for accessing these non-zero elements so that they can still be referred to by the usual (row, column) subscripts.*
2. *Discuss the criteria by which hashing functions are chosen and explain the need for overflow tables.*

3 Lists

Lists are part of our lives; we use them for shopping, remembering what to do, where to go and so on. It would be untrue to say that we always start at the top of a list and work down but it does happen sometimes. Very often it is just a case of crossing off an item on the list no matter where the item exists in the list. All in all, we take the amending of lists very much for granted, but if we are to represent information in a computer system using a list structure, we must also make sure that amending facilities are built into the structure.

In this chapter we will discuss exactly how list structures can be represented so that they are flexible enough to deal with the demands of inserting and deleting data within the structure.

3.1 Sequential lists

Stacks

Suppose a company has a number of employees whose work records are held in the company's computer system. A list of the employees' names is represented by the one-dimensional array in Fig. 16. The elements of the array occupy contiguous memory locations in the computer system and gaps are left at the bottom of the list so that the names of new employees can be added to the list.

The orders the company receives for its products never assume a steady level so employees have to be signed on and laid off as the fortunes of the company rise and fall. Consequently, the management of the company and the employees' union agreed upon the principle of 'last-in-first-out' when it came to dismissing employees. If this is the case, we can see from Fig. 16 that Soper was employed after Dupont but Beaver was employed before everyone else. This situation produces a list of a

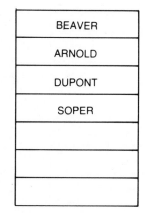

Fig. 16 A company's record of employees' names.

particular type called a *stack* which is generally represented by Fig. 17 rather than Fig. 16.

As its name suggests, items in the stack can only be accessed when they are on the top of the stack. In order to access the top of the stack, a *stack pointer* is used which must always be updated should the stack be amended.

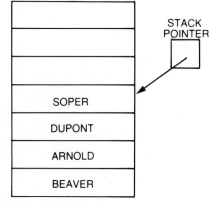

Fig. 17 A stack.

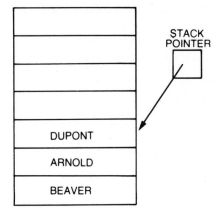

Fig. 18 The amended stack after deletion of the data SOPER.

The procedure of adding data to the top of the stack and updating the stack pointer is called *stacking*, whilst the removal of data from the top of a stack is known as *unstacking*.

The stack pointer contains the actual storage location of the data item at the top of the stack. For example, if Soper were to be dismissed, the data SOPER would be deleted from the list and the stack pointer would be amended to point to the data DUPONT as in Fig. 18.

The steps involved in stacking a data item are as follows:
1. Access stack pointer.
2. Increment stack pointer.
3. Store data item at location specified by stack pointer.

The steps involved in unstacking a data item are as follows:
1. Access stack pointer.
2. Transfer data at location specified by stack pointer to another location if required.
3. Decrement stack pointer.

Queues

An entrepreneur is building a large supermarket and is concerned as to

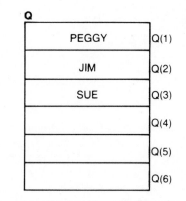

Fig. 19 Cash desk queue represented by a one-dimensional array.

how many cash desks he should install. He has commissioned a computer bureau which has the suitable software to solve his problem. The entrepreneur has given the bureau all the information concerning the cash desk procedures, including the fact that no more than six people may queue at any given cash desk.

One of the functions the computer bureau will aim to emulate with its software are these queues of no more than six people. One of these queues might well be represented by a one-dimensional array, Q, occupying six contiguous memory locations $Q(1)$, $Q(2)$, ..., $Q(6)$. The simulation of the cash desk queue would involve forming a queue as in Fig. 19.

Because change is taking place at both ends of the queue, i.e. customers are being served and more are joining the queue, the simulation must have two pointers indicating the start and finish of the queue as shown in Fig. 20.

Suppose Peggy and Jim are served, and Tom, Barbara and Sally join the queue. The start pointer must now indicate Sue to be at the head of the queue whilst the finish pointer must indicate Sally at the tail as in Fig. 21.

Notice that whilst the queue might have moved in real life, in our model there was no need to move all the data up two places because pointers were used to indicate the start and end of the queue. Suppose

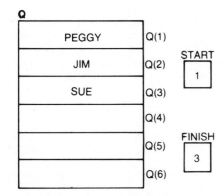

Fig. 20 The queue must have start and finish pointers.

one more person joined the queue, Brenda. The temptation would be to increase the size of our one-dimensional array Q to 7 so the data BRENDA could be referenced by Q(7). This method, however, is wasteful of computer memory particularly if a large number of customers are dealt with. The problem is solved by entering the data BRENDA into Q(1) because this element of the array is now unused since Peggy was served

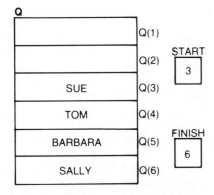

Fig. 21 The queue after two deletions and three additions.

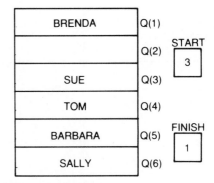

Fig. 22 The queue has a circular structure.

and left the queue. This action has created a circular list. Obviously the end-of-queue pointer would have to be amended as shown in Fig. 22.

The steps involved in adding data to a circular queue structure are as follows:
1. If the queue is full refuse entry.
2. Update the finish pointer so that it contains the address of the next available storage location to be used.
3. Store the data in the address specified by the finish pointer.

The steps in removing data from the head of a circular queue structure are as follows:
1. Copy the data found at the address specified by the start pointer so that the data can be used elsewhere.
2. Update the start pointer such that it contains the address of the new head of the queue.

Amending lists

Suppose a hospital computer system holds the medical records of all the patients being treated in the hospital. It may be that the patients' names are held in the one-dimensional array structure which is represented by Fig. 23, where the data occupies contiguous memory locations. The next free location could be indicated by a pointer so that when a patient is

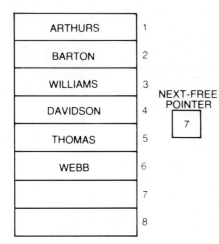

Fig. 23   Hospital patients' names could be held in a one-dimensional array.

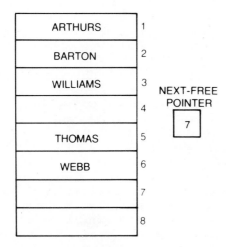

Fig. 24   Deletion of the data DAVIDSON.

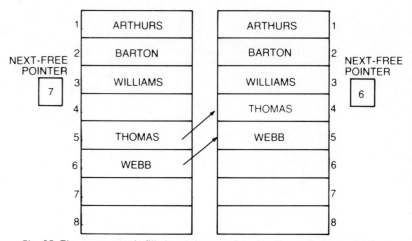

Fig. 25   The empty gap is filled and the next-free-location pointer amended.

admitted to hospital his or her name can be entered into this free location.

After treatment, the patient Davidson is discharged from the hospital and his medical records are removed from the computer system. This would cause two steps to be taken by the computer system; the first is the deletion of the data DAVIDSON from the list structure as in Fig. 24, and the second is the moving up of the data THOMAS and WEBB to make use of the unused gap as in Fig. 25. Obviously the next-free-location pointer would need updating as well.

We have taken a simple case here with only a few names being used as data, but with only a little imagination it can be seen that a computer system using the list structure as demonstrated would not cope efficiently with a large number of patients. The next section of this chapter shows a more realistic solution to the same problem.

The steps involved in adding data to a linear list structure are as follows:

1. Store the data at the address specified by the next-free pointer.
2. Update the next-free pointer to contain the address of the next free storage location.

The steps involved in deleting data from a linear list structure are as follows:

1. Find the data item to be removed from the list at position P in the list.
2. If the data item at position P is the last in the list, go to Step 6.
3. Transfer the data found at position P+1 in the list to position P.
4. Increase P by 1.
5. Go to Step 2.
6. Update the next-free pointer to contain the address of the storage location of position P in the list.

3.2 Linked lists

One-way lists

The example using a sequential list to hold the names of hospital patients highlights the restrictions sequential lists impose despite their undoubted worth when implementing stacks and queues. A more flexible concept is to think of a list as a set of *nodes* or items of data occupying non-contiguous memory locations but linked with one another through pointers. A linked list representation of Fig. 23 is shown in Fig. 26. Notice

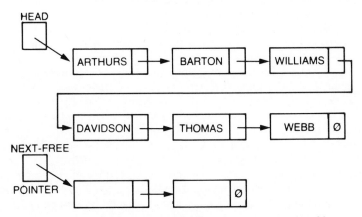

Fig. 26 A linked list representation of the patients' names from Fig. 23.

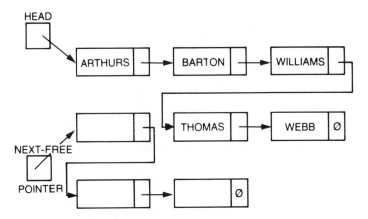

Fig. 27 The linked list of Fig. 26 after the node DAVIDSON has been deleted.

that the first node in the list is accessed by a pointer so that entry can be made to the data in the list; this pointer is called the *head* of the linked list.

Notice also that each node of the list consists of data and a pointer to the next node in the list. So, by following the pointers from the head of the list it is possible to access each node no matter where the nodes physically exist in the computer's memory, until the end-of-list pointer ϕ is found. It is worth noting that the next-free pointer is still in existence, pointing to the next free node which in turn points to the next.

The true benefits of such an arrangement are noticed when the linked list is amended. For instance, just as before, we wish to remove the data concerning the patient Davidson from the list. This requires that the data DAVIDSON be accessed and then deleted. The pointer to this node is then diverted to point to the node containing the data THOMAS which had previously been pointed to by the DAVIDSON node. The now empty node is made available to the next-free pointer. Hence the new representation as shown in Fig. 27.

As you can see, the changing of pointers has considerable advantages over the physical movement of data that was necessary using sequential lists, not the least of which is the saving of time. Another most important advantage is that the nodes of the list need not occupy contiguous memory locations, indeed they need not exist in the computer system's main memory but on some form of background memory, e.g. discs. However, it must be realized also, that linked lists in general do require more computer memory and a certain amount of housekeeping, i.e. changing of pointers, than do sequential lists. One other drawback, found particularly in the type described above, is that the random accessing of nodes is slow because a sequential search is required to access a particular item of data, whilst this can be done directly using the array structures described in the previous chapter.

The steps involved in adding data to a one-way linked list are as follows:
1. Starting at the head pointer, follow the node pointers through the list structure from node to node until the end of the list is found.
2. Transfer the contents of the next-free pointer to the node pointer previously specifying the end of the list.
3. Transfer the data which is to be added to the list to the node address specified by the next-free pointer.
4. Update the next-free pointer with the contents of the pointer associated to the recently added node data.
5. Set the pointer associated with the recently added node data to indicate end-of-list.

The steps involved in deleting data in a one-way linked list are as follows:
1. Starting at the head pointer, follow the node pointers through the list structure from node to node until the node to be deleted is found.
2. The redundant data was accessed through the pointer of the preceding node. Update this pointer with the contents of the deleted node's pointer.
3. Update the pointer associated with the redundant data with the contents of the next-free pointer.
4. Update the next-free pointer with the address of the deleted node's storage location.

Circular and two-way linked lists

One big disadvantage of using the linked list structure we have seen so far is that it is one-way, i.e. it is only possible to examine the data in the list from the top to the bottom and there is no going back to re-examine a node. This problem can be overcome by causing the pointer of the last node in the list, or the tail as it is sometimes called, to point to the head of the list thus making the list *circular* as represented in Fig. 28.

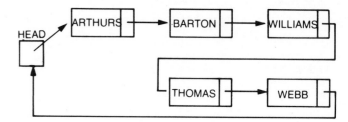

Fig. 28 The linked list of Fig. 27 can be made circular.

With this structure, each node can be accessed from every other node in the list but this can be slow if the list is long. One solution to this problem would be to introduce a second pointer which would link the nodes up the list instead of just down as before. This would make it possible to move in either a forward or backward direction from a node: a *two-way linked list* has been formed. This solution, has of course, a high overhead of storage requirements, and life becomes somewhat more complex when adjusting pointers to accommodate insertions and deletions to and from the list. The circular two-way linked list representation of our patients' names is shown in Fig. 29.

The memory overhead of the two-way linked list structure has been commented on, which prompts the question, 'Is it worth using this structure?' Again it comes back to our maxim mentioned in Chapter 1:

INFORMATION ≡ DATA + STRUCTURE

The structure chosen must, as we have discussed before, represent the information accurately and must also be flexible enough to allow the data to be amended without corrupting the information. Perhaps conflicting with this concept, the computer programmer has to implement the

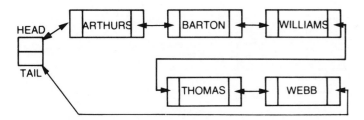

Fig. 29 The circular, two-way linked list representation of Fig. 27.

structure chosen without demanding so many of the computer system's resources that no one else can use the system effectively. Consequently, a compromise takes place. It makes sense to use structures which, where necessary, require a large number of pointers when the data at each node of a list is also large. In our examples, we have used nodes with just one record for data but it could have been several hundred records, the same principles apply.

So, in answer to the question, we could say 'Yes' if the amount of extra memory required for pointers is minimal compared with the overall amount of memory being used.

One further advantage of two-way linked lists is that it is possible to reconstruct most of the list should a node be lost due to a system malfunction, for example, in our hospital records model as represented in Fig. 29. Suppose the node containing the data BARTON were lost, by following the pointers from the head of the list forward and then backward it would be possible to reconstruct the rest of the list. If a one-way linked list structure had been used the nodes from BARTON and beyond would have been lost.

The steps involved in adding data to a two-way circular linked list are as follows:
1. Store the data at the address specified in the next-free pointer.
2. Update the backward pointer of this new node with the contents of the tail pointer.
3. Update the forward pointer of the node accessed through the tail pointer with the contents of the next-free pointer.

4. Update the forward pointer of the new node with the address of the tail pointer.
5. Update the tail pointer with the contents of the next-free pointer.
6. Update the next-free pointer with the address of the next free storage location.

The steps involved in deleting data from a two-way circular linked list are as follows:
1. Search the list following the forward or backward pointers for the node which is to be deleted.
2. Update the forward pointer of the node accessed through the backward pointer of the deleted node with the contents of the forward pointer of the deleted node.
3. Update the backward pointer of the node accessed through the forward pointer of the deleted node with the contents of the backward pointer of the deleted node.
4. Update the forward pointer of the deleted node with the contents of the next-free pointer.
5. Update the next-free pointer with the address of the deleted node.

3.3 Multiple linked lists

When representing the linked list structure in diagrammatic form the nodes of the list have been displayed as in Fig. 26 to emphasize the point that the nodes of the list can occupy non-contiguous memory locations. If we assume this point to be understood, we could re-represent the linked list structure in a tabular form. For instance, Fig. 29 represents a circular two-way linked list structure with names as data. A tabular representation of Fig. 29 could be as shown in Fig. 30.

The forward and backward pointers for a given node indicate the position in the list of the next node following or preceeding the node, and do not indicate the physical location of the node data in the computer system. The physical location of the node data could be determined by the use of several devices; access tables, stacks, queues, etc.

The most common use of linked lists as opposed to sequential lists is

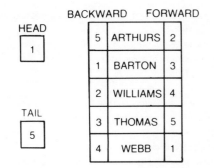

Fig. 30 Tabular representation of the circular two-way linked list.

in the processing of large amounts of data. This node data is normally not just a single field but is more likely to be a set of records, perhaps even a file.

Suppose that a college requested that all information concerning the students' academic work was to be represented on a computer system in such a way that the performance of students in their classes could be observed. A list structure could be used to represent this information within the computer system with the node data comprising a student's name, address, date of birth, grade and academic performance. In the diagrams which follow, the node data will be represented by the student's name only. In our example we will use data concerning the students Webster, Collins, Slater, Andrews and Martlew.

It is important to use a structure that will provide some form of back-up facility should any of the data at a node be lost. A two-way linked list provides this back-up as described in the previous section. Perhaps one of the most obvious ways of providing the two-way linked list is to sort the nodes into alphabetical order. This can be achieved without moving the node data but by setting up the pointers correctly as in Fig. 31.The alphabetical order pointers provide the same function as the forward pointers used in previous examples, whilst the reverse alphabetical order pointers replace the backward pointers.

One of the specifications laid down for this college computer system was that students' performances could be monitored. When the students

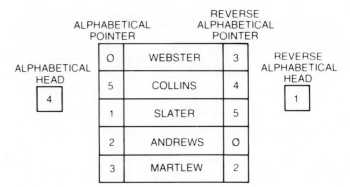

Fig. 31 Alphabetical pointers.

complete their examinations the college administrators want to find out the rank order of the students in each subject examined. Suppose that in one particular examination, say, history, the rank order of our students was Martlew, Collins, Andrew, Webster and finally Slater. Once this order has been established, the rank can be used to set up pointers in a list as shown in Fig. 32. Each node of the list had to be accessed and examined to build this new history rank list. Now, any enquiries concerning the rank order of students in history are made through this new list and the actual accessing of student nodes is minimized.

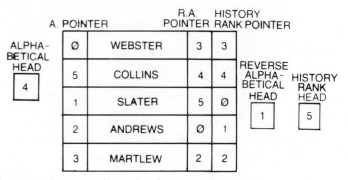

Fig. 32 Using pointers to order students' exam results.

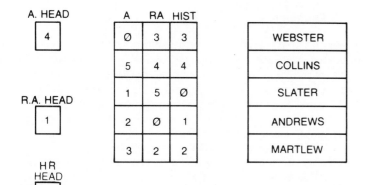

A. HEAD

4

R.A. HEAD

1

H R
HEAD

5

A	RA	HIST
Ø	3	3
5	4	4
1	5	Ø
2	Ø	1
3	2	2

WEBSTER
COLLINS
SLATER
ANDREWS
MARTLEW

Fig. 33 Node data and pointers may be kept in separate files.

The tabular representation of the linked list structure in Fig. 32 does not show clearly what happens in practice. Because of the large amount of node data, i.e. student records, it is most likely that this node data will be held in one file whilst the associated pointers are held in another file in the computer system. Perhaps a better representation would be as in Fig. 33.

Very often the file containing the pointers is held in the computer system's main memory so that it can be accessed almost immediately to ensure a quick response to enquiries.

Summary

After reading this chapter, the reader may have arrived at the conclusion that linked lists are vastly superior to that of sequential lists. This may be so, but it must be remembered that the purpose of using a structure is to accurately represent the relations which exist in reality, so in some cases the so called 'simple' sequential list in its various guises of stack and queue can also be superior.

Programmers have in the past found difficulty in representing complex relationships using lists. This is not just because these relationships are complex but because they change and the programming amendments required to re-structure the representation prove to be considerable. As a result, list processing languages such as LISP and SNOBOL have been developed to allow programmers to solve programming problems without worrying about the building of data structures for the data to live in.

EXERCISES
1. a. Describe how the information in the BASIC declaration
       100 DIM X (12,20)
       is used by the BASIC system in the execution of the statement
       200 LET A(5,12) = A(12,5)
       Show clearly any calculations performed by the system.
   b. Discuss the suitability of
       (i) a one-dimensional array and
       (ii) a linked list, for implementing a stack in a high-level language
       Say in each case how an empty stack would be represented.
       (London 1977)
2. A directory exists for the files stored on a disc. This directory also contains entries for the extensions to some of these files.
   Describe the structure you would use to represent file information in this directory including the facility for file extensions.
   Describe how your structure copes with the addition and deletion of files to or from the disc and how free disc space is monitored.

4 Trees

The linear structures we have used so far have only allowed us to show that each node is related to the preceding and succeeding nodes in the list. This restricts us to representing relationships based on a single criteria. However, in many cases, structures are required to represent the hierarchical relationships between nodes. In particular cases this can still be achieved using a linear list, e.g. the rank order of students' examination results, but what happens if more than one student achieves the same result? The linear list is unable to cope with such a problem. In such an instance a *tree* structure is used.

This chapter discusses the special vocabulary associated with tree structures, the various forms of trees, their implementation and their limitations.

4.1 Tree terminology

If the Earth's land masses with the continents and countries were to be represented in hierarchical order the diagrammatic representation might well be as shown in Fig. 34. Admittedly, not all the countries in each continent are shown but a few have been illustrated as being representative. From Fig. 34 it can be seen that the Earth consists of several land masses, Africa, North America, etc., which are comprised of various states or countries.

Throughout the rest of this book, references are going to be made to nodes that exist within tree structures. References will be in the form of node DATA, which means that the node consists of a set of pointers and the data DATA. For example, in Fig. 34 we could refer to node NORTH AMERICA which indicates that we are discussing the node at which the data NORTH AMERICA can be accessed.

The representation in Fig. 34 is called a tree because when the representation is inverted it bears a resemblance to a tree. The analogy is continued; in our diagram the *root* of the tree is the node EARTH whilst the lines connecting the nodes are called *branches*. A node in our example such as BRAZIL is called a *terminal node* or a *leaf*.

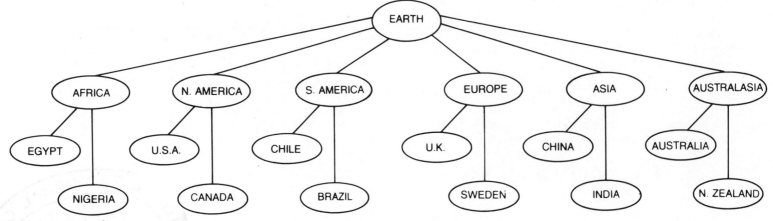

Fig. 34 An example of a tree structure.

A further analogy is that likening our representation to a family tree, where the descendants of a node are called *children* and the immediate ancestor to a node is called a *parent node*. The left child node of a parent node is defined as the *eldest child*. For a tree structure, each node has a parent node, except of course, the root of the tree.

A *subtree* consists of a parent node with children nodes, whilst the *degree* of a node is the number of subtrees which exist from that node.

Particular subtrees which exist within a tree structure can be referenced individually. For example, the term 'the subtree AFRICA' can be used to reference the node AFRICA (in Fig. 34) and its children nodes, node EGYPT and node NIGERIA.

The *level* of a node is the lowest number of nodes that have to be passed through, including the root of the tree, to gain access to the node. For instance, in Fig. 34 the level of node CANADA is 3.

We have, in fact, been using a special case of a tree structure in the use of lists. An example of this special case is shown in Fig. 35 where the root of the tree is the node WEBSTER and the terminal node is the node MARTLEW.

There are several other names given to particular types of tree structure. A *balanced tree* is a tree where each parent node of the tree has the same number of children. Obviously, an *unbalanced tree* is similar to our example in Fig. 36 where not all the nodes have the same number of children. A special case of a balanced tree is a *binary tree* where each node has exactly two children, except of course, the terminal nodes. This special case and some of its applications will be discussed later in Chapter 5.

4.2   Accessing the nodes of a tree

Because tree structures are by definition complex, it is important that an efficient method of accessing the nodes of a tree, or *traversing* as it is called, is found. So that the methods described below can be compared, the tree represented in Fig. 36 will be used as a test bed.

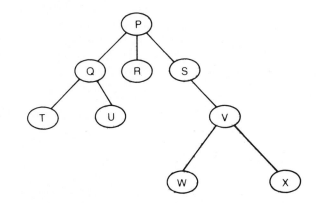

Fig. 36 This tree is used here to test various forms of traversal.

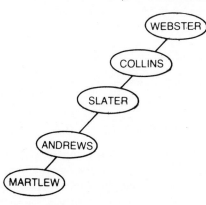

Fig. 35 Lists are really a special case of the tree structure.

Level-by-level traversal

Perhaps one of the most obvious methods of accessing the nodes would be to start at the root of the tree, P, and work down to the terminal nodes, level by level, from left to right. This method would cause the nodes to be accessed in the following order:

P Q R S T U V W X

The steps involved in a level-by-level traversal are as follows:
1. Access the root of the tree on level 1.
2. Increase the level number by 1.
3. If there are no nodes at this new level then finish.
4. Access the nodes at this new level from left to right.
5. Go to Step 2.

Pre-order traversal

This method has proved popular with the implementors of database systems which use tree structures to represent the complex relationship requirements of information. Database systems allow vast amounts of data to be interpreted, related and processed in a variety of ways. Some of the methods used in organizing the necessary structures are described in Chapter 6.

The first node to be accessed is the root of the tree, P, followed by the leftmost branch node of the structure Q. The children of Q are then accessed from left to right, T and U. With these two terminal nodes accounted for, the next branch node from the root is accessed, R, which itself is a terminal node. Finally, the last branch node from the root is found, S, followed by its child, V, and its children from left to right, W and X which are terminal nodes.

So, using this method, the nodes are found in the following order:

P Q T U R S V W X

where the parent nodes are always accessed before their children nodes.

The steps involved in pre-order traversal are as follows:
1. Access the root node.
2. Access the eldest child of the currently accessed node.
3. If the currently accessed node is a parent node then go to Step 7.
4. If the next eldest twin node of the current node exists, access it and go to Step 3.
5. If the stack is empty then finish.
6. Unstack a node pointer and if this node's next eldest twin node exists, access the next eldest twin node and go to Step 3, otherwise go to Step 5.
7. Stack a pointer to the current node and go to Step 2.

Suffix walk

This method differs from those previously mentioned because the tree structure is attacked from its terminal nodes and not through its root so that the children are accessed before their parents.

As before, the traverse works from left to right but starts this time with the leftmost terminal node T, moves across to its brother U, then to the parent node Q. Still working from left to right, the node R is accessed as it is a terminal node. The next terminal node is W followed by X which exhausts the terminal nodes so that their parent node V is found. Following the branch back from node V, S is found to be the rightmost child of the root P which is now accessed.

The order in which the nodes are traversed is as follows:

T U Q R W X V S P

The steps involved in the suffix walk are as follows:
1. Access the leftmost terminal node.
2. If the currently accessed node has no younger brother nodes then go to Step 4.
3. If the younger brother node is a terminal node then access it and go to Step 2, otherwise locate this younger brother node and go to Step 6.
4. Access the parent node of the currently accessed node. When the root of the tree is found—finish.
5. Go to Step 2.
6. Locate the eldest child node of the currently located node.
7. If the currently located node is a terminal node then access it and go to Step 2, otherwise go to Step 6.

4.3 Representation of trees in a computer system

In this section two methods are discussed to show how tree structures are represented in a computer system. By using the same tree structure and the same example for both methods it is hoped that the reader will be able to see clearly the advantages and disadvantages of both methods.

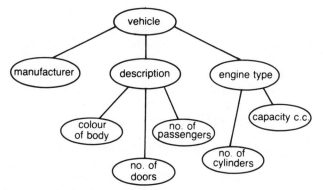

Fig. 37 Motor vehicle specifications.

Let us take for our example a tree structure that might be used in a database system which is to be interrogated concerning the specifications of motor vehicles. The structure we will be using is shown in Fig. 37. The structure might well be a subtree from a much larger tree but that is not our concern at the moment. Fig. 38 shows just one of the possible occurrences for our motor vehicle structure.

There are two possible methods of representing this example: the data can be stored sequentially or in a linked list form.

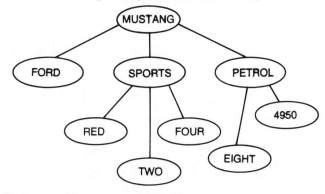

Fig. 38 One possible occurrence of Fig. 37.

Sequential processing of a tree

First of all, we will assume that the structure in Fig. 38 is traversed; the pre-order traversal is used so that the sequential representation of this appears in Fig. 39. Remember that the data stored here is occupying contiguous memory locations.

Fig. 39 Sequential representation of Fig. 38 after pre-order traversal.

One important point must be realized here which again goes back to what was being discussed in Chapter 1.

INFORMATION ≡ DATA + STRUCTURE

The data sequentially listed in Fig. 39 is just data until the structure represented in Fig. 37 is applied to it, otherwise the data could be misinterpreted. For instance, the data TWO and FOUR could be understood to mean the vehicle seats two passengers and has a four cylinder engine.

As we have seen before in the previous chapter, sequential lists have the advantage of being easy to use and implement. However, there are

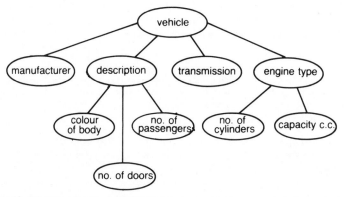

Fig. 40 'Motor vehicle specifications' tree structure amended to include transmission specification.

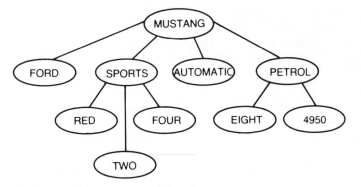

Fig. 41 One possible occurrence of Fig. 40.

two major drawbacks: firstly to access a given node in the tree it is necessary to access the nodes sequentially until the node is found, and secondly the inserting or deleting of nodes causes all the node data to be re-written. Both of these are severe handicaps to a system if the tree contains many nodes, for example, if the structure specified in Fig. 37 were to be amended to that in Fig. 40 by the inclusion of a transmission specification. An occurrence of the new structure could be shown in Fig. 41. This relatively small amendment to the tree structure would have considerable consequences; the structure in Fig. 41 would have to be traversed and a new sequential representation produced as shown in Fig. 42.

MUSTANG	FORD	SPORTS	RED	TWO	FOUR	AUTOMATIC	PETROL	EIGHT	4950

Fig. 42 New sequential representation as a result of including transmission specification.

The steps involved in the insertion or deletion of data in the occurrence of a tree structure are as follows when the structure is represented sequentially:

1. Amend the tree structure as required.
2. Traverse the whole tree according to the algorithm for traversal, to produce sequential representation.

Linked list processing of a tree

When using a linked list to represent a tree structure it is necessary for two pointers to be associated with each node of the tree. The first pointer indicates the first child of a node, i.e. the leftmost child, and the second pointer indicates the presence of a child of the same parent, i.e. a twin pointer. A linked list representation of Fig. 38 is shown in Fig. 43. The symbol ϕ is used to indicate the end of a chain of pointers.

The insertion and deletion of nodes does not require the rewriting of the node records as was the case with sequential listing of a tree. For instance, if it were necessary to add a node to the structure concerning say, the colour of upholstery in a vehicle, this would require the structure described in Fig. 37 to become that of Fig. 44. If the colour of upholstery in our example is to be white, the node WHITE would have to be introduced; the twin pointer of node RED would be amended to point to node WHITE, and the twin pointer for WHITE would assume the previous value of RED's twin pointer. This new representation is shown in Fig. 45.

Deleting a node from the list is equally trivial. For instance, if it was decided to dispense with the record specifying the number of doors the car had, i.e. node TWO, then the twin pointer of the preceding node in the

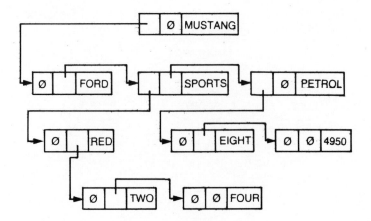

Fig. 43 A linked list representation of Fig. 38.

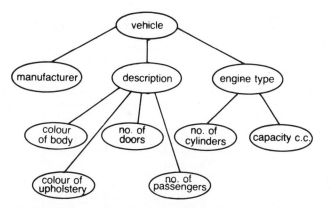

Fig. 44 'Motor vehicle specifications' tree structure (Fig. 37) revised to include 'colour of upholstery'.

chain, node WHITE in this case, would have to assume the value of node TWO's twin pointer.

One further advantage of the linked list structure over the sequential list is that it is possible to access a node without having to pass through every node in the tree, e.g. to access node PETROL in Fig. 45 only nodes

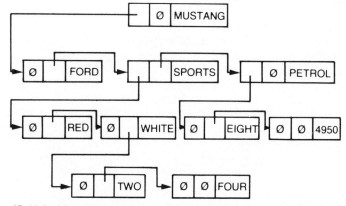

Fig. 45 Linked list representation revised to include 'colour of upholstery'.

MUSTANG, FORD and SPORTS must be read whereas before nodes RED, WHITE, TWO and FOUR would also have to be read.

The steps involved in adding a node to a linked list tree structure are as follows:
1. Traverse the tree following the node pointers until the new node's elder twin is found.
2. Set the new node's twin pointer to contain a copy of its elder twin's twin pointer.
3. Amend the elder twin's twin pointer to contain the address of the storage location of the new node.

The steps involved in deleting a node from a linked list tree structure are as follows:
1. Traverse the tree following the node pointers until the node to be deleted is found.
2. If the node to be deleted has an elder twin then amend the twin pointer of the elder twin to contain a copy of the twin pointer of the deleted node.
3. If the node to be deleted has no elder twin then amend the child pointer of its parent node to contain a copy of the deleted node's twin pointer.

The tree structure in Fig. 45 can be represented in tabular form as in Fig. 46. The previous representation (as in Fig. 45) has been used to emphasize the point that the nodes of a tree need not occupy contiguous memory locations.

The amending of these linked lists is as we have seen reasonably straightforward but there are some drawbacks. Suppose the tree structure we have been using is interrogated and the node being accessed is node FOUR (see Fig. 46). As the structure exists at the moment the pointers used to gain access to this node must be remembered, perhaps in a stack, so that it is possible to trace the pointer back along the chain to the parent node, SPORTS. To overcome this problem, the end-of-the-chain markers can be changed to point to their twin at the head of the chain so that circular lists are formed to enable every node to be accessed from every other node. These new pointers are shown in Fig. 47.

INDEX	NODE DATA	CHILD POINTER	TWIN POINTER
1	MUSTANG	2	Ø
2	FORD	Ø	3
3	SPORTS	4	8
4	RED	Ø	5
5	WHITE	Ø	6
6	TWO	Ø	7
7	FOUR	Ø	Ø
8	PETROL	9	Ø
9	EIGHT	Ø	10
10	4950	Ø	Ø

Fig. 46 Tabular form of Fig. 45.

INDEX	NODE DATA	CHILD POINTER	TWIN POINTER
1	MUSTANG	2	Ø
2	FORD	1	3
3	SPORTS	4	8
4	RED	3	5
5	WHITE	Ø	6
6	TWO	Ø	7
7	FOUR	Ø	4
8	PETROL	9	2
9	EIGHT	8	10
10	4950	Ø	9

Fig. 47 Using end-of-chain markers.

Summary

The tree, as we have seen, is an extremely useful structure when hierarchical relationships are to be represented; however, it is the representation of a tree structure inside a computer system that demands a great deal of thought. It would make little sense to implement the sequential processing of a tree structure if the data in the structure had to be amended frequently. Consequently, most, although not all, tree structures are represented in a linked list form.

EXERCISES
1. Construct a tree which represents the structure of this book with its chapters and sections.
   Devise a method of representing this tree structure in a computer system using arrays such that the title of a chapter or section can be found by supplying the chapter or section reference.
2. Construct your own family tree tracing your ancestry as far back as you can through the male or female side of your family.
   Represent this tree structure in a computer system in such a form that when the tree is traversed, all your ancestors of a particular generation are grouped together.

5 Binary Trees

In the previous chapter, reference was made to a particular form of tree data structure called a *binary tree*. The methods involved in traversing, representing and building binary trees are discussed in this chapter.

Suppose that a credit company held records concerning the credit-worthiness of its clients, in alphabetical order in a computer system. These records must be available for inspection quickly so that enquiries concerning clients can be dealt with efficiently. The clients' records might be held in a linear list structure in a sequential manner as shown in Fig. 48. However, as we have discussed before in Chapter 3, this structure does not allow the records to be accessed efficiently. A more commonly used structure is the binary tree. The binary tree representation of the credit company records (using the data in Fig. 48) is shown in Fig. 49.

Notice that the root node TYSON was taken from the middle of the list in Fig. 48, whilst its children nodes, BARNES and WILLIAMS were taken from the middle of the top and bottom halves of the list. The ways in

| AMBLER |
| BARNES |
| FREDERICKS |
| TYSON |
| WATSON |
| WILLIAMS |
| YULE |

Fig. 48 A credit company's records of its clients.

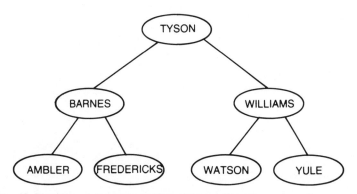

Fig. 49 The binary tree representation of the credit company records.

which binary trees are built are discussed later in this chapter. In this example of a binary tree we can see that any child node to the left of a parent node is higher in alphabetical order than its parent node, whilst the child node to the right is lower in alphabetical order.

It can be seen that nodes existing in a binary tree structure can be accessed more quickly than those in a sequential linear list. For example, node YULE can only be found in Fig. 48 by accessing all the other nodes in the list, but in Fig. 49 only nodes TYSON and WILLIAMS need be accessed to find YULE.

5.1 Traversing binary trees

Binary trees can be traversed using the methods described in Chapter 4 but if the reader applies those methods he will note that none of them allows the nodes of the tree in Fig. 49 to be accessed in alphabetical order. One method which does work is to start at the leftmost terminal node AMBLER, traverse to its parent node BARNES and then to its twin node FREDERICKS. This has caused the subtree BARNES to be traversed. If we now move to the root of the tree TYSON, the right-hand subtree WILLIAMS can be traversed in a similar manner as subtree BARNES, i.e. WATSON, WILLIAMS and YULE. The order in which the nodes are traversed is shown in Fig. 50. The detailed method by which this traversal is achieved is discussed later on in this chapter.

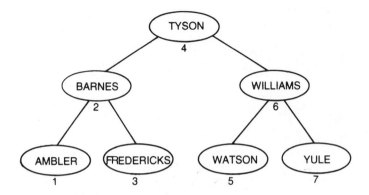

Fig. 50 The order in which the nodes are traversed.

5.2   Representation of binary trees in a computer system

In our definition of a binary tree we said that every node in such a tree had two children, except of course the terminal nodes which have none. We have also seen the advantages of using nodes with links, so to represent a binary tree we will use nodes with two pointers, LEFT and RIGHT, which will point to the left and right children of a node respectively. Consequently, the binary tree represented in Fig. 49 can be represented as in Fig. 51.

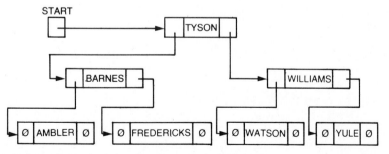

Fig. 51 The linked list representation of Fig. 49.

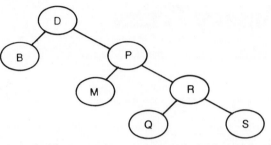

Fig. 52 The root of a binary tree does not have to be in the middle of the list of expected data.

Searching for a node

The accessing of a particular node, say WATSON, requires access to be made initially to the root of the tree via the start pointer. Comparison is then made between the sought after data WATSON, and TYSON. Because WATSON is alphabetically lower than TYSON the right pointer is followed to node WILLIAMS. Again a comparison is made and as WATSON is higher than WILLIAMS the left pointer is followed to node WATSON.

It is not critical that the root of the binary tree is a node containing data which is in the middle of the list of expected data as can be seen from the representation in Fig. 52. The nodes in this example are letters of the alphabet and the structure arranged them in alphabetical order. When this structure is implemented, the nodes will require left and right pointers as illustrated in Fig. 53.

The steps involved in searching for a particular node in an ordered binary tree are as follows:
1.   Access the root of the binary tree using the start pointer.
2.   If the data at the currently accessed node is equal to the data of the node being sought then finish.
3.   If the current node is a terminal node then the node sought after does not exist in this tree.
4.   If the data at the current node is less than the data of the sought

after node then follow the right pointer of the current node, otherwise follow the left pointer of the current node.

5. Go to Step 2.

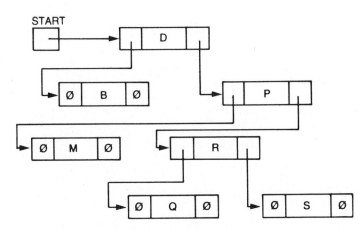

Fig. 53 The linked representation of Fig. 52.

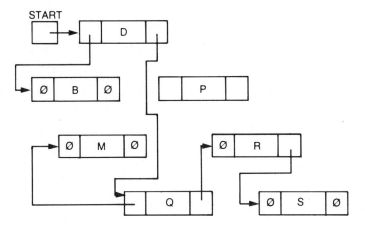

Fig. 54 Deleting node P.

Deleting nodes

If it is necessary to delete a node from such a tree the problem is trivial if the node to be deleted is a terminal node; its parent's pointer to the deleted node is set to ϕ, the null pointer. However, the problem is considerably more complex if, say, node P is to be deleted. If such a node is to be removed, a replacement must be found which retains the logical order of the tree. A search is first made by following P's right pointer to R. The replacement for P must be the leftmost terminal node in the subtree R, which in this case is node Q. Several pointers now have to be amended; the right pointer at root D must point to node Q, the left and right pointers of Q must assume the values of the left and right pointers of P, and the left pointer of R must be set to ϕ, the null pointer. The new representation is shown in Fig. 54. The result as we can see is not a strict binary tree but the nodes are still ordered.

The steps involved in deleting a particular node from an ordered binary tree are as follows:

1. Access the node to be deleted from the tree.
2. If the currently accessed node is a terminal node set its parent node's pointer to null and finish.
3. Access the node indicated by the right pointer of the current node.
4. If this newly accessed node is a terminal node go to Step 6.
5. Access the node indicated by the left pointer of the current node and go to Step 4.
6. Amend the left pointer of this terminal node to contain a copy of the deleted node's left pointer.
7. Amend the right pointer of this terminal node to contain a copy of the deleted node's right pointer unless this causes the right pointer to point to its own node in which case it is set to null.
8. Amend the pointer of the deleted node's parent node to contain the address of the storage location of this terminal node.
9. Finish.

Inserting nodes

The insertion of nodes into a binary tree structure is relatively straightforward and the method used is really an extension of that used to search an ordered binary tree. If, for example, a node N were to be inserted into the binary tree as represented in Fig. 53 the new node could only be introduced as a child node to one of the existing terminal nodes in the structure. The solution for this insertion involves traversing through the structure via node D and node P until node M is accessed. Node M is found to be a terminal node and the node data M is greater than the data N so the right pointer of node M is amended to contain the address of the storage location of node N. The left and right pointers of node N are set to null as it is a terminal node. This new representation is shown in Fig. 55.

The steps involved in inserting a node into an ordered binary tree are as follows:

1. Access the root of the binary tree using the start pointer.
2. If the data at the current node is the same as that of the new node then insertion need not take place. Finish.
3. If the node currently being accessed is a terminal node then go to Step 6.
4. If the data at the node currently being accessed is less than the data at the new node then follow the right pointer of the current node, otherwise follow the left pointer of the current node.
5. Go to Step 2.
6. If data of the new node is less than the data of the current node then amend the left pointer of the current node to contain the address of the new node's storage location, otherwise amend the right pointer in a similar manner.
7. Set the left and right pointers of the new node to null.
8. Finish.

5.3 Accessing a binary tree in order

Earlier in this chapter, a method of traversing a binary tree was briefly discussed where the nodes of a tree could be accessed in alphabetical order. We are now going to deal with the implementation of that method in detail and discuss the associated problems.

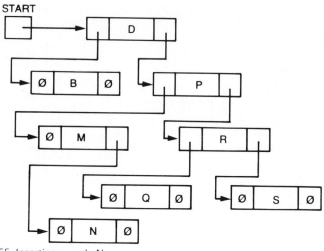

Fig. 55 Inserting a node N.

Suppose that we wish to list the nodes of the tree in Fig. 56 in alphabetical order. By using the start pointer, access to the root of the tree is made from where the leftmost terminal node can be accessed. Obviously the data at node D can now be listed but a problem now exists because there is no pointer at node D to return to the next node to be output, node F. Consequently, we arrive at the conclusion that a stack must be used to retain the address of node F so that the data at node F, and eventually the data at node J, can be listed.

To explain the operation of the stack, the tree in Fig. 56 has been expanded by introducing some more nodes as shown in Fig. 57. The table

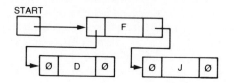

Fig. 56

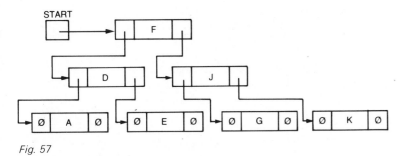

Fig. 57

	node currently accessed	node listed	stacked pointers to nodes	
			top	bottom
1	F			
2	D		F	
3	A	A	D	F
4	D	D	D	F
5	E	E	D	F
6	D		F	
7	F	F		
8	J			
9	G	G	J	
10	J	J		
11	K	K		

Fig. 58 Listing the nodes of the tree in Fig. 57.

in Fig. 58 shows contents of the stack and the nodes listed at each step as the structure in Fig. 57 is traversed.

As before, entry is made to the tree via the START pointer (Step 1). In order to access the leftmost terminal node A, we have to make two entries in the stack; the first is a pointer to the root node F (Step 2) and the second is a pointer to node D (Step 3), the parent of node A. Once the data at node A has been output, the pointer at the top of the stack is used to gain access to node D (Step 4). The pointer is retained at the top of the stack so that after node E has been accessed (Step 5) it can be used to return to node D and then removed from the stack (Step 6). The pointer at the top of the stack now allows us to return to the root of the tree, F (Step 7).

The right pointer of the root node is now followed to node J (Step 8). there is no need to stack the address of the root because the data at that node has already been listed and there is no need to return there. From node J we move to the leftmost terminal node stacking the address of J (Step 9). At node G the data is listed and then the return address at the top of the stack is used to return to J (Step 10). The remaining terminal node K can now be found using the right pointer of node J (Step 11). The table in Fig. 58 describes the procedure of listing the nodes of the tree in Fig. 57.

The reader should have noticed by now that the subtrees to the left and right of the root node are treated in exactly the same way except that when traversing the right-hand side of a tree, the return address pointers are not stacked after the node has been listed. Nodes J and F are examples of this.

The above method has an obvious drawback in that a stack has to be

START

INDEX	LEFT POINTER	NODE DATA	RIGHT POINTER	PARENT POINTER
1	2	F	5	Ø
2	3	D	4	1
3	Ø	A	Ø	2
4	Ø	E	Ø	2
5	6	J	7	1
6	Ø	G	Ø	5
7	Ø	K	Ø	5

Fig. 59 Parent pointers can be used instead of a stack.

introduced and manipulated; one way round this problem is to introduce a third pointer at each node which points to the parent of each node. This new representation can be seen in tabular form in Fig. 59.

The addition of a pointer to the parent node relieves us of the problem of using a stack but there are two disadvantages. The first is that there is no means of telling whether the data at a node has been listed. This problem arises when dealing with parent nodes which are accessed more than once. This could be solved by introducing yet another pointer associated with each node, but a simpler method would be to set the parent node pointer positive initially and change its sign when the node has been listed. The second disadvantage of using a parent node pointer is that some nodes on the right-hand side of the tree, e.g. J and K, will not use these pointers.

This third pointer could also be used if the tree is to be traversed frequently in such a way that the nodes are in order. It would be much more efficient if this third pointer were used to indicate the next node to be accessed rather than just the parent node. Using this technique, the tree represented in Fig. 57 could be re-represented in tabular form to give Fig. 60. The first node of the ordered tree is accessed via the trace pointer and from there on, each node can be accessed in order by following the trace pointers at each node. This structure, known as *threaded list*, is

INDEX	LEFT POINTER	NODE DATA	RIGHT POINTER	TRACE POINTER
1	2	F	5	6
2	3	D	4	4
3	Ø	A	Ø	2
4	Ø	E	Ø	1
5	6	J	7	7
6	Ø	G	Ø	5
7	Ø	K	Ø	Ø

Fig. 60 Trace pointers indicate the next node to be accessed.

easier to implement than the previous two methods, however, the implementor must weigh against the advantages of this method the fact that extra storage space is required.

The steps involved in listing the node data of a binary tree in order with the use of a stack are as follows:
1. Access the root node of the binary tree using the start pointer.
2. If the currently accessed node is a terminal node go to Step 7.
3. If the left pointer of the current node is null go to Step 10.
4. Put the address of the current node at the top of the stack.
5. Access the node pointed to by the left pointer of the current node.
6. Go to Step 2.
7. List the current node data.
8. If the stack is empty then finish.
9. Access the node whose address is at the top of the stack and remove this address from the stack.
10. List the current node data.
11. If the currently accessed node has a null right pointer go to Step 8.
12. Access the node pointed to by the right pointer of the current node.
13. Go to Step 2.

5.4 Building ordered binary trees

So far we have discussed how to implement and use binary trees to represent relationships. However, the degree of success of these structures depends largely on how well the tree was built in the first place. The efficiency with which individual nodes in a tree can be accessed depends upon the efficiency of the method used and on the representation of the tree structure. We have already discussed at length the methods used for accessing nodes so we will now discuss the representation of a tree structure.

Suppose we were to take the nodes AUSTRALIA, CANADA, NEW ZEALAND, SOUTH AFRICA, UNITED STATES OF AMERICA (U.S.A.)

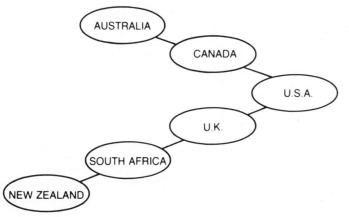

Fig. 61

and UNITED KINGDOM (U.K.) and build a tree such that the alphabetical order of the nodes was represented. The representation produced, would depend entirely on the order in which the nodes were presented during the building of the tree. Fig. 61, Fig. 62 and Fig. 63 show three different

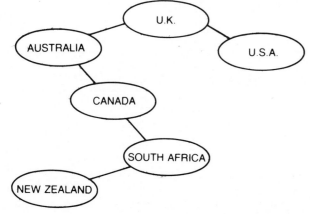

Fig. 62

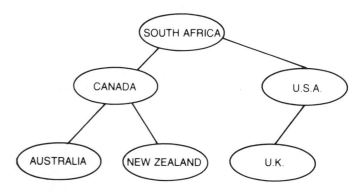

Fig. 63

representations of tree structure each with the nodes in the order in which they were submitted. Each tree is built by taking the first node submitted and using this as the root node. Each subsequently submitted node is compared with the root node and its children until its appropriate position is found. As can be seen there is a considerable difference between the diagrammatic representations of these trees; Fig. 61 shows us that a list is formed.

If the tree representations were to be compared to see how efficient they are in terms of accessing individual nodes, the representation in Fig. 61 would come off worst, as one would expect, whilst the representation in Fig. 62 is only marginally better. Only in Fig. 63 do we find a representation which gives us an efficient structure for examining nodes. So, it can be seen that whilst it is not mandatory, it is desirable for the root of a binary tree to be at or near the middle of the order of nodes.

The steps involved in the building of an ordered binary tree are the same as those for the insertion of nodes, the method for which has been described earlier in this chapter. There is, however, one important difference. The insertion method works on the basic assumption that there is a tree structure into which a node can be inserted. Obviously when a tree is built, there is nothing there to start with so the very first node submitted for insertion into this empty tree must become the root of the tree and be made accessible using the start pointer. Every other node submitted from there on is inserted into the new tree according to the method mentioned earlier.

Summary

The tree is used to represent the hierarchical relationships between nodes of data and can be implemented in many versions as we have seen. Not all the uses of binary trees have been discussed but this special case, the binary tree, is used again in Chapter 7 on simple syntax analysis.

EXERCISES

1. *A publisher maintains a list of his books currently in print. Each book is represented in the list by its standard book number. The list is maintained in ascending numerical order of code numbers, and is updated by inserting and deleting entries for books as they are published or become out of print.*

   Discuss the suitability of sequential storage in a one-dimensional array structure (or vector) for computer storage and processing of this information.

   Describe by means of diagrams and written explanation, an alternative storage structure using links (pointers).

   For the alternative storage organization you have described, give detailed instructions for effecting each of the following operations:
   (a) deleting a book number as the book becomes out of print, and freeing the space which becomes available,
   (b) adding the book number of a newly published book.
   Take care to allow for the case of a book number which precedes all those currently on the list. Take all possible steps to ensure that the attempted addition of a new book number does not fail while unused storage exists.
   (LONDON 1975)

2. *A knock-out tournament has 16 competitors; matches are played between two competitors and the winner goes on to the next round, where again players are paired. Eventually, a single winner emerges. Show how this may be represented by a binary tree, and draw a flowchart to extract and print the competitors who played against the eventual winner of the tournament.*
   (A.E.B. 1977)

3. *The rules for sorting a list of integers using a binary tree are as follows:*
   (i) take the first integer as the data element at the root,
   (ii) compare the next integer with the element at the root; if it is greater it is placed on the right at the next level, otherwise on the left,
   (iii) for each subsequent integer in the list the process described in (ii) is repeated with comparisons continuing through the tree until a vacant position is found.
   a. Using these rules construct a sort tree for the list
   36, 75, 26, 92, 36, 23, 20, 46, 33.
   b. Describe an algorithm which will retrieve the sorted list of data from the tree.
   c. If it is known that the data contains many repeated items, suggest an improvement to the rules above.
   d. What characteristic of the initial data list would cause this sorting method to become particularly inefficient?
   (Cambridge Specimen Paper)

6 Networks

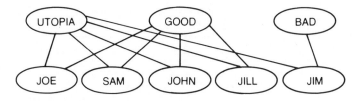

Fig. 65 A possible representation of Fig. 64.

The tree structure described in the previous chapter represents the hierarchical relationships which exist between nodes which have only one parent. The *network* structure makes it possible to represent relationships between nodes with several parents.

This chapter discusses the different types of network structures that exist, their implementation and their limitations.

6.1 Simple and complex networks

Simple networks

Suppose the situation of the election of a single state representative were to be illustrated as a network structure, the result would be as shown in Fig. 64. Each voter must be a citizen of the state in order to use their one vote to elect a representative. The relationships between the voter and the state and between the voter and the candidate are both one-to-one. This means that the voter in this representation has two parents. On the other hand, the state has many citizens, i.e. voters, and the candidate has many of these voters so the relationships between the state and the voter and the voter and the candidate are one-to-many.

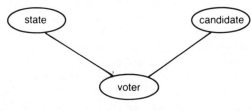

Fig. 64 A simple network.

If a network exists such that a one-to-many relationship exists in one direction only then this is called a *simple network*.

A representation of the simple network in Fig. 64 is shown in Fig. 65 where there are two candidates GOOD and BAD. Notice that each voter, JOE, SAM, JOHN, JILL and JIM has two parents, the state UTOPIA and either a GOOD or a BAD.

Complex networks

If people were allowed to become members of several sports clubs and this was represented diagrammatically, a *complex network* would be the result as shown in Fig. 66. Each sports club has several members, some of whom may belong to other sports clubs. Consequently, a one-to-many relationship exists in both directions: from member to clubs and from club to members.

A network with one-to-many relationships in both directions is called a *complex network*.

An example of the complex network in Fig. 66 is shown in Fig. 67

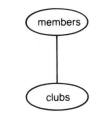

Fig. 66 A complex network.

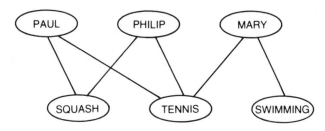

Fig. 67 An example of the complex network in Fig. 66.

where PAUL is a member of the SQUASH and TENNIS clubs, PHILIP is a member of the TENNIS and SQUASH clubs and MARY is a member of the TENNIS and SWIMMING clubs.

6.2   Representation of networks

Sequential lists

The technique to produce sequential lists can best be described by using the network in Fig. 67 as our example. It involves reducing the network to a *forest* of trees or separate trees with roots PAUL, PHILIP and MARY as shown in Fig. 68.

Notice that this reduction produces nodes which appear more than once in the forest. The node TENNIS for instance, appears in all three trees. The trees are now traversed so that a sequential list can be made of

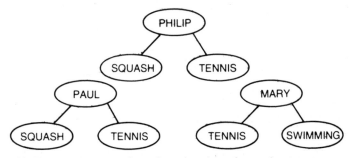

Fig. 68 The complex network can be reduced to a forest of trees.

| PAUL | SQUASH | TENNIS | PHILIP | SQUASH | TENNIS | MARY | TENNIS | SWIMMING |

Fig. 69 A sequential list formed after pre-order traversal of the trees in Fig. 68.

the nodes. The pre-order traversal method has been used on the trees in Fig. 68 to produce Fig. 69. In previous chapters of this book we have discussed the poor facilities available to help with the amending of sequential lists, but as can be seen in this particular implementation of a network, the sequential list is not a worthwhile proposition because of the amount of node duplication. Do not forget that whilst we have used nodes consisting of one record, the nodes could be somewhat larger and this technique would eat hungrily and greedily into a computer system's memory resources.

The steps involved in representing a network in the form of a sequential list are as follows:
1. Separate the network into a set of trees, the roots of which are the parent nodes in the network.
2. Traverse each tree in turn using an appropriate traversal method to produce a sequential list.

Linked lists

The linked list is probably the most commonly used structure for the implementation of networks both simple and complex. We will use the example in Fig. 67 again so that a direct comparison can be made between the sequential list and the linked list techniques.

Each member in Fig. 67 would contain a pointer to every club the person is a member of. Similarly, each club node would contain a pointer to each of its members. This situation is represented in Fig. 70.

The reader should have noticed a few points here: perhaps the most obvious is that Fig. 70 looks messy because of the number of pointers required, and also that some of the nodes require more pointers than others. The problem of the messy representation can be overcome by presenting Fig. 70 in a tabular form as shown in Fig. 71. This tabular form not only looks tidier but also emphasizes the point made earlier concerning the number of pointers required for each node. In most of the

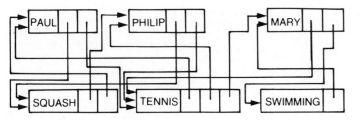

Fig. 70 The linked list representation of Fig. 67.

ENTRY NO.	NODE	POINTERS		
1	PAUL	4	5	
2	PHILIP	4	5	
3	MARY	5	6	
4	SQUASH	1	2	
5	TENNIS	1	2	3
6	SWIMMING	3		

Fig. 71 The tabular form of Fig. 70.

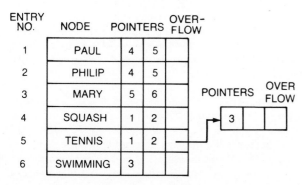

Fig. 72 Overflow pointers can be used if needed.

cases, the third pointer space is unused which prompts the question of its existence. But what about the node TENNIS? The third pointer cannot be ignored so special facilities have to be developed such as using overflow pointers to a list of spare pointers. This would require each node to contain an overflow pointer, most of which will be unused in this example. The tabular representation of the nodes with the usual two pointers plus an overflow pointer is shown in Fig. 72.

The overflow pointer of node TENNIS indicates that further pointers can be found at the location specified. Notice that the set of two spare pointers has its own overflow pointer so that if need be more pointers could be accommodated.

In our example we have used a maximum of two pointers before the overflow pointer is employed. In reality, this would create high demands on memory with the use of overflow pointers so the technique should be used in a manner which allows a majority of the nodes to be accessed without the use of an overflow pointer.

The steps involved in representing a network in the form of a linked list are as follows:
1. Access a root node of the network.
2. Store the root node data.
3. Traverse the subtree to access the child nodes of the root node.
4. At each child node, store the node data, set a root node pointer to the child node data and set a child node pointer to the root node data.
5. Go to Step 1 unless all the root nodes in the network have been accessed.

6.3   A compromise in the representation of networks

We have just seen that sequential lists are capable of representing both simple and complex networks but that they have a severe disadvantage in that some nodes are duplicated. Similarly, linked lists deal with both types of network quite well except that the manipulation of pointers becomes somewhat complex, and techniques have to be devised to cut down the amount of memory the pointers consume, e.g. overflow pointers.

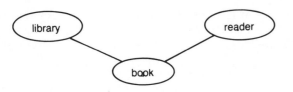

Fig. 73 A simple network.

Eventually a compromise can be reached using a combination of sequential and linked lists—but at a cost. The technique can only cope with simple networks. The complex networks are best dealt with using linked list procedures.

To explain this technique we will represent the simple network structure as shown in Fig. 73. This is a simple network because each book has two parents; a book belongs to one library and is read by one reader at a time so that relationships here are one-to-one. In the other direction, a library has many books and a reader can use several books at one time so these relationships are one-to-many. An example of this network structure is shown in Fig. 74 where library L1 has books B2 and B4, whilst library L2 has books B1, B3, B5 and B6. Reader R1 reads books B3, reader R2 reads books B2 and B4 whilst reader R3 reads books B1, B5 and B6.

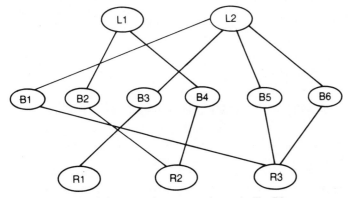

Fig. 74 An example of the network structure shown in Fig. 73.

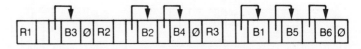

Fig. 75 A sequential representation of the reader nodes and book nodes in Fig. 74.

Part of this representation can be re-represented sequentially; usually this is the largest number of nodes associated with two of the three types of node available: library, book and reader. In this case the reader nodes and book nodes are chosen and represented sequentially with links in Fig. 75. Associated with each book node is a pointer indicating the whereabouts of a twin node, and with each reader node there are two links, one is used as a child pointer and the other is kept free at this stage. The null pointer ϕ indicates the end of a chain of nodes. Finally, the library nodes are represented sequentially each with a pointer indicating the position in the first list of the first child node. Some book node pointers in the first list have to be amended to allow the relationships between library and books to be represented.

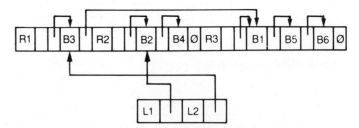

Fig. 76 The introduction of library nodes causes the twin pointer for node B3 to be amended.

At this stage, difficulties can be experienced by gaining access to the child nodes of a reader node, i.e. book nodes. The recent amending of the null pointers in Fig. 75 to twin pointers in Fig. 76 could give the false impression that reader R1 has access to not only book B3 but also B1, B5 and B6. To overcome this problem, the free pointer associated with each reader node could be used to hold the number of book nodes available to that reader. This solution is shown in Fig. 77.

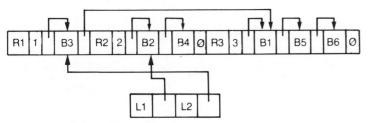

Fig. 77 A complete representation of Fig. 74.

The steps involved in representing a network using a combination of sequential and linked lists are as follows:

1. Determine the two types of nodes which are most frequently found in the representation of a network and which are to be represented sequentially.
   (The two types are usually a set of root nodes and a set of child nodes.)
2. Access the root of a subtree.
3. Store the node data sequentially allowing space for two pointers.
4. Traverse the subtree from the root node. As each node is accessed, store the node data sequentially allowing space for one pointer.
5. When the first node of the subtree is accessed, set the second pointer at the root node to this node.
6. Set the node pointers to their twin node unless there are no more in which case this pointer is set to null and the first pointer at the root node is set to the number of child nodes from that root.
7. Go to Step 2 if there are more root nodes of the same type, else go to Step 8.
8. Determine which nodes have yet to be accessed. (They usually belong to a set of root nodes.)
9. Access the root of a subtree. This root belongs to the set of nodes determined in Step 8.
10. Store the node data sequentially allowing space for one pointer.
11. Traverse the subtree from its root and as each node is accessed, search for its node data in the first sequential list which was created in Steps 1 to 7.
12. When the data of the first node in the subtree has been found in the sequential list set the root node pointer in the second sequential list to this location.
13. When the node data is found in the sequential list the pointer of the node is amended to point to the current node's twin node. If the current node is the last node in the subtree then this pointer is set to null.
14. Go to Step 9 unless there are no more root nodes of the same type.

Summary

Of the three methods of implementing a network discussed in this chapter, the linked list is the most commonly used despite the complexity of its pointer management. This method scores over sequential lists, which require the duplication of some nodes, and over the combined sequential and linked list method which cannot cope with complex network structures.

EXERCISES
(see page 42)

EXERCISES

1. *In a given hospital each patient is allocated a bed in a ward and a particular doctor; the relationships look like this:*

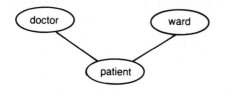

Is this a simple or complex network?
Represent this network in a suitable form in a computer system using the following occurrence:

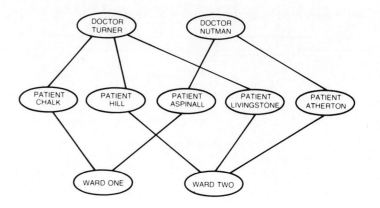

7 Simple Syntax Analysis

The term 'syntax analysis' can be used to describe any process which attempts to determine whether or not some data obeys a particular convention thus producing information. The data 'The boy ate an orange' can be analysed syntactically according to the rules for the structure of an English sentence. No errors in the syntax of the data would be forthcoming and so the data would be judged to be an English sentence, presumably imparting some information to the reader. If the data 'an orange' were replaced by the data 'a building' the syntax analysis of the data would produce no errors because a noun has been replaced by another noun under the rules of English grammar. The presumption then, that because our data is syntactically correct an English sentence exists which must provide us with meaningful information, must be queried.

This point raises the question of the purpose of syntactic analysis of data. Data is analysed syntactically to ensure that the data adheres to certain conventions which are the axioms on which procedures have been developed to process the data.

In this chapter we will discuss the methods and structures used in the syntax analysis of arithmetic expressions and how the result of this analysis—*reverse Polish notation*, is used to evaluate expressions.

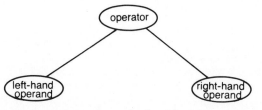

Fig. 78 A tree structure representing a simple arithmetic expression.

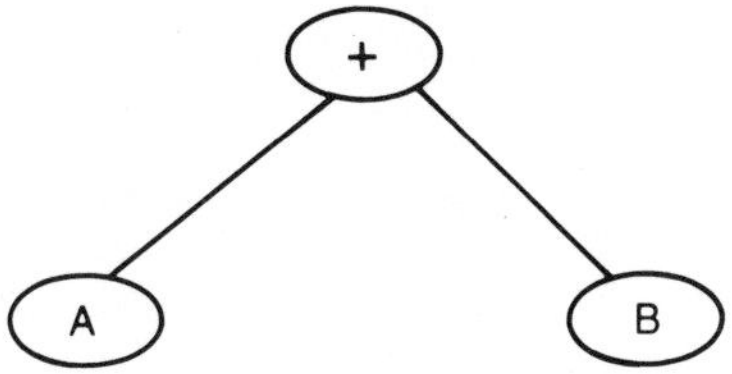

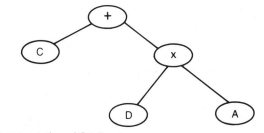

Fig. 79 Representation of A + B.

7.1 Polish notation

Building trees

Let us look first of all at a very simple arithmetic expression, e.g. A + B. The expression consists of three items; the left-hand operand A, the operator + and the right-hand operand B. This relationship can be represented by a tree structure as in Fig. 78. The operator is shown to be the parent node of the two operand nodes. In our example, we used the operator + and operands A and B as in Fig. 79.

So far we have chosen a very simple arithmetic expression as our example. Suppose we used a more complex example such as $C + D \times A$. A problem now exists as to how we can represent this in the form of a tree. According to our structure in Fig. 78 we must use an operator as our root node, but in this case we have two, + and ×. We know through our experiences in mathematics that multiplication and division must be performed before addition and subtraction. This convention means that the result of $D \times A$ must be evaluated first before it can be added to C.

Fig. 80 Representation of $C + D \times A$.

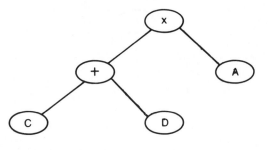

Fig. 81 Representation of (C + D) × A

Consequently, the operator × will have to be a child node to the node +. Our tree representation of C + D × A looks like Fig. 80.

However, if we take the same expression, C + D × A and amend it slightly to become (C + D) × A, we change the order in which the expression is evaluated. The presence of the brackets indicates that the sum of C and D must be multiplied by A so we must make the node + a child node to the node × as in Fig. 81.

In the above examples, we have used binary trees to illustrate the role of binary operators in arithmetic expressions. There are times, however, when unary operators, those with only one operand, are used, e.g. (−P + 2) × (S + T). Here, there are three binary operators +, × and + and

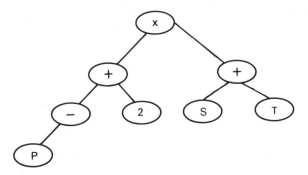

Fig. 82 Representation of (−P + 2) × (S + T)

only one unary operator −. The presence of the brackets causes the node × to be the root node of the tree representing this expression (See Fig. 82). The child nodes of the root node × are the two + nodes. The right-hand + node subtree appears in a similar form as in previous examples. The left-hand + node subtree has as its left operand a chain of nodes − and P to represent the term −P.

Consequently, we arrive at the convention for representing binary and unary operators in a tree structure; binary operator nodes have two children nodes and unary operator nodes have only the one child node.

The steps involved in building a binary tree to represent an arithmetic expression are as follows:
1. Scan the arithmetic expression for a binary operator with the lowest precedence. When it is found, create the root node of the tree with the operator as data.
2. The arithmetic expression has now been split into two new expressions: the left- and right-hand parts, both of which are treated in a similar manner.
3. If the current arithmetic expression contains a binary operator go to Step 6.
4. Create a terminal node with the operand as data.
5. If more expressions are to be analysed go to Step 3, else finish.
6. Scan the arithmetic expression for a binary operator with the lowest precedence. When found, create the root node of a subtree of the structure 'operand, operator, operand' with the operator as data.
7. Go to Step 2.

Traversing binary trees

In Chapter 4 we discussed the various methods of traversing trees. The results of a tree traversal in this context are of considerable importance as we shall see later in this chapter.

Suppose we traverse the tree represented in Fig. 79 according to the pre-order traversal method; the result would give us + A B. This would mean that the operator + must act on the operands A and B. This notation is sometimes called *Polish prefix notation* because the form was devised

ROOT L R

by a Polish mathematician called Lukasiewicz. The term 'prefix' is used to denote that the operator is a prefix to the operands.

If we apply the same traversal method to the tree represented in Fig. 80 we would obtain + C × DA. If this Polish prefix notation is to be translated back into a form which is more easily understood, a technique has to be devised to perform the translation. Perhaps the best method is to work from the end of the string of characters back towards the front. By grouping the characters in such a way as to emphasize the relationships between operator and operands, we can derive the expression C + D × A. Scan the character string from right to left until the first operator is found, this gives us × D A and D × A when translated. This expression must be an operand of another operator, and so the scan continues until another operator is found and the complete expression can be translated to give C + D × A.

This method has its disadvantages in that the whole Polish prefix expression has to be input before any translation into a normal arithmetic expression (infix notation) can be performed. If the same tree representation, Fig. 80, were to be traversed using the suffix walk method, described in Chapter 4, then the result would be C + D A ×. This expression is in *Polish suffix notation* or *reverse Polish notation*. The term suffix is used to show that the operator always appears after the operand.

7.2   Syntax analysis using reverse Polish notation

In the next two sections the following symbols will be used to denote operators; + addition, − subtraction, × multiplication, / division and ↑ exponentiation. Through our experience of mathematics we have discovered that some arithmetic operators have to be acted upon before others so a hierarchy of operators exists. The hierarchy we are going to use is given in Fig. 83.

( ) highest precedence

↑

x /

+ − lowest precedence

Fig. 83 The hierarchy of arithmetic operators.

We will discuss in this section a means of analysing an arithmetic expression in infix notation and translating it into reverse Polish notation so that it can be evaluated. The next section of this chapter describes how a reverse Polish expression is evaluated.

Suppose we wish to convert the infix notation of H − C / P ↑ 2 + G into reverse Polish notation. One method would be to produce a tree representation of the infix notation as in Fig. 84 and traverse the tree using the suffix walk. The tree in Fig. 84 is built using the method described earlier in this chapter.

The expression H − C / P↑2 + G is scanned until the binary operator + is found to have the lowest precedence; the operator, −, could be used equally as well but the operator + is the most recently accessed if the scan works from left to right through the expression. Consequently the root of the tree is the node +.

The character to the right of the operator + is dealt with easily as it is an operand and so the terminal node G is formed.

The expression to the left of the operator + is also scanned for an operator of lowest precedence and the node − is formed as a result. This node, −, now forms the root of a subtree which represents the arithmetic expression H − C/P↑2. The operand, H, to the left of operator − is represented simply by the terminal node H.

The expression C /P↑2 is now scanned and the operator / is found to

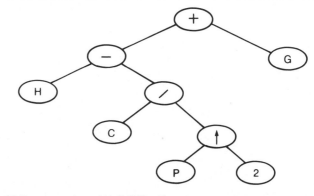

Fig. 84 Representation of H−C/P↑2 + G

have the lowest precedence causing the root of the subtree / to be formed. The operand C is represented easily with node C, as is the expression P↑2 which is represented as the right branch node to the node / .

The result of the suffix walk would give the reverse Polish expression HCP2↑/−G+.

An alternative approach would be to devise an algorithm to perform the conversion from infix to reverse Polish notation. Using our example of H−C/P↑+G we shall proceed to perform the conversion. The procedure described below is represented in Fig. 85. The infix notation string H−C/P ↑2+G is input character by character. As the first character is a variable, H, it is output immediately (Step 2). The second character, −, is input and stacked, as it is an operator and we require its right-hand operand before it is output (Step 3). The next character, C, is input and output immediately (Step 4).

We have now input two variables and one operator, and the

temptation is to output the operator to complete the expression but the second operand might not be complete.

The next character is input and is found to be an operator. This second operator, /, is stacked as it has a higher precedence than the operator − currently at the top of the stack (Step 5). In other words, there is still an operand to be input. The character P is now input and output immediately as it is a variable (Step 6). When the next character, ↑, is found to be an operator, it is stacked as it has a higher precedence than the operator at the top of the stack, / (Step 7).

The next character input, the constant 2, is output (Step 8) and the operator + is accessed. At this point, the operator at the top of the stack, ↑, has a higher precedence than the operator + so the ↑ is output (Step 9) followed by / and − (Steps 10 and 11). This takes place because the operator at the top of the stack at any time must have a lower precedence than the input operator. The operator + is now placed in the stack.

The final character, the variable G, is input and then output (Step 12) followed by the contents of the stack (Step 13).

The above technique deals with arithmetic expressions containing binary operators but many arithmetic expressions contain brackets which cause the order of operations to be changed.

Let us take the infix notation B × (2 + C) − D and represent this in the form of a tree. The resulting tree is found in Fig. 86. If this tree were to be traversed using the suffix walk method the resulting reverse Polish expression would be B2C+×D−. Notice that this expression does not contain any brackets.

	Input Characters	Character Accessed	Output Characters	Stack top		bottom
1	H−C/P↑2+G					
2	−C/P↑2+G	H	H			
3	C/P↑2+G	−	H	−		
4	/P↑2+G	C	HC	−		
5	P↑2+G	/	HC	/	−	
6	↑2+G	P	HCP	/	−	
7	2+G	↑	HCP	↑	/	−
8	+G	2	HCP2	↑	/	−
9	G	+	HCP2↑	/	−	
10	G	+	HCP2↑/	−		
11	G	+	HCP2↑/−	+		
12		G	HCP2↑/−G	+		
13			HCP2↑/−G+			

Fig. 85 The procedure for converting H−C/P↑2+G from infix notation to reverse Polish notation.

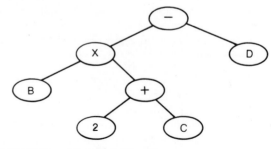

Fig 86 Representation of B × (2 + C) − D.

	Input Characters	Character Accessed	Output Characters	Stack top	bottom
1	B × (2 + C) − D				
2	× (2 + C) − D	B	B		
3	(2 + C) − D	×	B	×	
4	2 + C) − D	(	B	(	×
5	+ C) − D	2	B2	(	×
6	C) − D	+	B2	+ (	×
7	) − D	C	B2C	+ (	×
8	− D	)	B2C+	(	×
9	− D	)	B2C+	×	
10	D	−	B2C+×		
11	D	−	B2C+×	−	
12		D	B2C+×D	−	
13			B2C+×D−		

Fig. 87 The procedure for dealing with brackets when converting from infix to reverse Polish notation.

We shall now discuss an algorithm for dealing with a string of characters in infix notation containing brackets. The whole of this procedure is represented in Fig. 87.

The first character input, B, is a variable and is output immediately (Step 2). The operator × is found next and is stacked (Step 3). The following character, (, is stacked (Step 4) as it has a higher precedence than the operator ×. The constant 2 is output (Step 5), but the operator + is compared with the operator at the top of the stack, (. When the operator (was stacked, it lost its high precedence and was reduced to an operator of the lowest precedence. Consequently, the + operator is stacked on top of operator ((Step 6).

The next character, C, is input and is output (Step 7) as it is a variable, however, the following character,), is regarded as an operator with a very low precedence. This causes the + operator at the top of the stack to be removed from the stack and output (Step 8). The matching left-hand bracket is also removed from the top of the stack and the matching brackets are then discarded completely to leave only the operator × in the stack (Step 9). The operator − is now input which causes the operator × to be removed from the stack and output (Step 10), and the − is stacked (Step 11). Finally, the variable D is input and output immediately (Step 12) followed by the operator − from the stack (Step 13).

The above algorithm depends heavily on being able to lower the precedence of the left-hand bracket after it has been stacked. In practice, this is performed by allocating priorities to all operators, including brackets, and reducing the priority of the left-hand bracket to a level as low as the lowest operator.

The two algorithms described above provide facilities for converting data in infix notation into reverse Polish notation but we must not become complacent. Built into these algorithms would have to be checks to ensure that the infix notation was syntactically correct. Data such as $A + \times C \uparrow D$ would be an obvious candidate for error reporting since it would be relatively easy to build into the algorithm a trap for receiving two successive operators, the second of which is not a unary operator such as + or −.

In our second algorithm we say that when a right-hand bracket was found, its matching left-hand bracket was removed from the stack. Such data as $(A + B \times C − D$ could be analysed and the missing right-hand bracket could be reported by checking the stack for the spare left-hand bracket after the last character has been input. Such checks as these could and should be built into a syntax analysis algorithm.

The steps involved in converting infix notation into reverse Polish notation are as follows:
1. Input a character—if there are no more left go to Step 11.
2. If the character is an operand output it and go to Step 1.
3. If the character is a left bracket, reduce its priority to the lowest level, stack it and go to Step 1.
4. If the character is a right bracket then reduce its priority to the lowest level.
5. If the operator at the top of the stack has a lower priority than the new character go to Step 9.

6. If the operator at the top of the stack is a left bracket remove it from the stack and go to Step 1.
7. Remove the operator from the top of the stack and output it.
8. Go to Step 5.
9. Stack the new character unless it is a right bracket.
10. Go to Step 1.
11. If the stack is not empty remove the operator from the top of the stack and output it, otherwise finish.
12. Go to Step 11.

7.3   Evaluating expressions in reverse Polish notation

If we were to represent the arithmetic expression $G + 2 \uparrow D/A$ in the form of a tree we would obtain a result as shown in Fig. 88. Suppose we were given values for the variables such that $G = 7$, $D = 3$ and $A = 4$. We would then be able to evaluate the expression, but as this expression is not just a matter of operand, operator, operand we will use the tree representation in Fig. 88 to help us. This tree with the values for the variables entered is shown in Fig. 89.

One way of using the tree is to traverse from left to right starting at the root. However, at the root, we find that whilst the left-hand operand 7 is available for immediate use the right-hand operand has yet to be evaluated as it is an operator with its own operands. The right-hand subtree at node / has to be traversed until a parent node can be found with

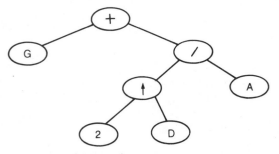

Fig. 88 Representation of $G + 2 \uparrow D/A$

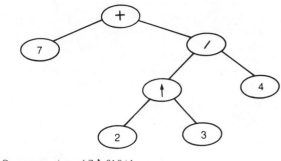

Fig. 89 Representation of $7 + 2 \uparrow 3/4$

two terminal nodes, or in other words, a subtree which can be evaluated. The subtree $\uparrow$ is one such as this, from which the result is 8. This can now be used to evaluate the subtree / to give the value 2. Finally, we have arrived at a situation where the root node + can operate on its two operands 7 and 2 to give the result of the expression 9.

It is worth noting the order in which the nodes of the tree in Fig. 89 were operated on was $7\ 2\ 3\ \uparrow\ 4\ /\ +$. This order is indicated in Fig. 90 by a sequence number alongside each node. The order in which the nodes are operated on is the same as if the tree had been traversed using the suffix walk method. This traversal method, as we discussed earlier, causes the nodes of a tree to be accessed in an order which is the same as that of the

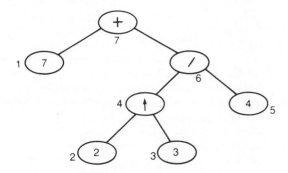

Fig. 90 The order in which the nodes of Fig. 89 are operated on.

characters in a reverse Polish expression. Now it is possible to see why it was necessary to convert an expression in the infix notation to reverse Polish notation in the previous section. When an arithmetic expression is presented for evaluation in reverse Polish notation it is already in a form which causes the algorithm for evaluation to be reasonably straightforward.

Let us assume that our arithmetic expression $G+2{\uparrow}D/A$ has been submitted to our syntax analysis algorithm of the previous section and the reverse Polish expression $G2D{\uparrow}A/+$ has been the result. If the values of the variables used are $G=7$, $D=3$ and $A=4$ we have the reverse Polish expression $723{\uparrow}4/+$ which has to be evaluated. The evaluation of our expression is shown in Fig. 91 step by step. The expression is accessed character by character from left to right.

When the operands 7, 2 and 3 are submitted they are stacked one by one. (Steps 2, 3 and 4). However, when the operator ↑ is input (Step 5) it is allowed to operate on the two operands at the top of the stack, 3 and 2, to give the result 8 which is retained at the top of the stack.

The operand 4 is now input and placed at the top of the stack (Step 6) so that when the operator / is input the new value at the top of the stack becomes 2 (Step 7) as a result of the operator / operating on operands 4 and 8.

Finally, the operator + is allowed to operate on the remaining two operands in the stack to give a result of 9 at the top of the stack (Step 8). The value of the expression is extracted from the top of the stack when the end of the expression has been found.

The steps involved in evaluating a reverse Polish expression are as follows:
1. Input a character—if there are no more the value of the expression is at the top of the stack.
2. If the character is an operand, stack it and go to Step 1.
3. If the character is a binary operator go to Step 5.
4. Remove an operand from the top of the stack, perform the operation on the operand, stack the result and go to Step 1.
5. Remove two operands from the top of the stack, perform the operation on these two operands, stack the result and go to Step 1.

	Expression being accessed	Stack		
		top		bottom
1	$723{\uparrow}4/+$			
2	$23{\uparrow}4/+$	7		
3	$3{\uparrow}4/+$	2	7	
4	${\uparrow}4/+$	3	2	7
5	$4/+$	8	7	
6	$/+$	4	8	7
7	$+$	2	7	
8		9		

Fig. 91 The procedure for evaluating $7+2{\uparrow}3/4$

Summary

We have seen that syntax analysis is used on data to ensure that defined structures are adhered to. Perhaps one function of syntax analysis which is sometimes overlooked is the necessity for a syntax analysis algorithm to not only detect errors but also report them in a manner that can be easily understood.

In our particular case of the analysis of arithmetic expressions we saw that a further function of a syntax analysis algorithm was to convert data in infix notation to reverse Polish notation so that the evaluation of the expression is a simpler task.

EXERCISES
1. *A first attempt to define a portion of the syntax of a programming language dealing with expressions involving only variables is made as follows:*

    <expression> → <variable> | <expression> <op> <expression>

    <op>   →+|*|↑

    <variable>   →A|B|C|D

Show that this is unsatisfactory, by drawing two different syntax trees for the expression

$$A*B + C \uparrow D$$

Subsequently, this inherent ambiguity is removed by replacing the definitions above by:

$<expression> \rightarrow <term> | <expression> + <term>$
$<term> \qquad \rightarrow <factor> | <term> * <factor>$
$<factor> \qquad \rightarrow <primary> | <factor> \uparrow <primary>$
$<primary> \qquad \rightarrow <variable>$
$<variable> \qquad \rightarrow A|B|C|D.$

a. Using a tree derived from the revised syntax rules, express
$A*B + C \uparrow D$
in reverse Polish (postfix) notation.

b. What change would you make to the definition of $<primary>$ to allow for bracketed expressions in this language?

(LONDON 1976)

2. Convert the following infix expression to postfix (reverse Polish) form:
$(A \times B - C \times D)/(A \times A + B \times B)$
Write down the infix string corresponding to the following postfix expression:
$3VP - / 4UP - / +$
(LONDON 1975)

3. A subroutine has been written to convert arithmetic expressions in infix notation into reverse Polish notation. The original expression is held in an array A and the new expression in an array B.

a. What limitations might one expect to find specified for the use of the subroutine? Explain why each is necessary.

b. Explain how such a subroutine should be tested and design some appropriate test data.

(LONDON 1978)

Index